Free
Degrees

**White Lion
Press**

This book is dedicated to Jan Dunn, former director of the Belgrade Youth Theatre, for making our teenage years a scream and giving us the feeling that we could do anything.

Many thanks also to Nessa and Susan Bassnett for their invaluable support and advice and to Richard Adams for his generous insight into the US education system.

Free
Degrees

How to fund your own education,
without debt

by Lyndi Smith

**White Lion
Press**

Published by
The White Lion Press Limited
567 Ben Jonson House
The Barbican
London
EC2Y 8NH
United Kingdom

© 2009 Lyndi Smith/The White Lion Press Limited
ISBN 978-0-9553993-1-2
All rights reserved

First printed 2009

No part of this publication may be reproduced, stored in a retrieval system,
or transmitted, in any form or by any means, electronic, mechanical, photocopying, recording, or otherwise, without the prior permission of the author
or publisher.

British Library Cataloguing-in-Publication Data.
A catalogue record for this book is available from the British Library.

Design and print production by em associates, London

Printed and bound in the United Kingdom by Bell and Bain Ltd

Contents

The author

Lyndi Smith is a freelance writer and associate director of Mad Half Hour Theatre Company, based in the UK. In 1998 she was accepted onto the acting course at the Royal Academy of Dramatic Art in London and raised over £26,000 to fund her studies.

For the past ten years, much of Lyndi's work has been with young people: in schools and youth theatres, with disadvantaged young people, or young people at risk of exclusion. She has performed in Hungary, India, at the National Theatre of Great Britain and has taught masterclasses in improvisation and Shakespeare in Luxembourg.

She has also created the website degreesforfree.com, which is a valuable resource for students everywhere.

Lyndi grew up on the stage of the Belgrade Theatre, Coventry as part of the Belgrade Youth Theatre. Lyndi writes, directs and produces plays and still lives in the same house she grew up in with her two cats, Pawsy and Mr Dylan.

Free Degrees is her first published title.

Preface

In 1998 I was offered a place at a top acting school in London. I was thrilled. It took me two years to get in, auditioning alongside four thousand others for only a handful of places. After my final audition, I went back home to Coventry and told myself I hadn't got in. I was preparing for the worst. If I was rejected, there could be no disappointment. If accepted, then it would be even more amazing.

If you are selected for a place, you receive a phone call within forty-eight hours. So when the phone rang and I recognised the principal's voice, I knew what it meant: success. I was over the moon.

I raced into Coventry town centre to find my friends. Everyone was delighted for me. The school had a reputation second to none and I was guaranteed the very best training money could buy.

At which point came the question:

'How are you going to get the money?'

I didn't know, then. I just believed that I would. That if I persevered, and asked enough people and really fought for it, I would somehow raise the cash I needed to pay for my training.

Over the next two years I raised everything I needed. I didn't have to take out a loan, get a job, or sell my body. The money came, from over three hundred different sources, sometimes in trickles and then at other times in great waves.

This book will show you how I did it.

It will also show you how to do it too.

Author's note

This book has evolved over the years from *Fundraising for Drama Students*, into *Fundraising for Students* and now as *Free Degrees*.

Although I trained in the UK in theatre, the lessons contained in this book are beneficial to everyone trying to raise money for their own education anywhere in the world. In rewriting, I have tried to make this book as internationally friendly as possible.

Mostly I have taken out all of the British-isms, but look carefully and you will notice the odd pound sign and reference to English theatre. There are extra notes and appendices throughout for residents of the USA, Canada, Australia and South Africa.

I hope these notes are sufficient to make this guidance relevant to your own country.

x

Chapter one

First things first

Get yourself a place on your chosen course

Before you begin to worry about where the money is coming from, concentrate on getting a place at your chosen school or university. This means choosing the course that is right for you and finding out about the selection process.

If you are unsure of which course to take, general information and advice can be obtained from your local careers service or library.

Details of all courses nationally are sometimes collated into handbooks, directories, or viewbooks. In the United Kingdom, you will need the *Universities and Colleges Admissions Service (UCAS) Handbook*; in the United States you should either contact each college for a copy of their viewbook or use the *Princeton Review*.

Each educational institution will be able to send out printed information on the courses offered and all colleges will be able to advise you on their selection procedure and approach to funding. Contact the college and ask to speak to the financial aid department or bursar's office. The staff there can advise you further on funding your education.

You may be entitled to support from the local or national authorities. The financial aid departments of each university or college can point you in the right direction. In the United Kingdom, you should contact your local education authority to see if you are able to apply for a grant before you have the definite offer of a place. *See* chapter two for more details on contacting your local education authority.

If you have been short-listed for an interview, find out as much as possible about the course and costs involved before you go. You may then be asked about how you intend to pay for the course.

If you are ineligible for any kind of grant or loan, don't worry. I wasn't entitled to any official financial support from the government or local authority and still managed to fund my further education. People will help when they see what a wonderful opportunity you have and you will get the money. Honestly. You will have to be dedicated and hard-working to raise the tuition fees and living costs but you can do it.

Turn yourself into a fundraiser

Before you continue reading, be advised: this is not a journey for the faint-hearted. You will definitely need the following: *perseverance, a fighting spirit, support from the people around you, a little luck, a dash of creativity, hard work, clear intentions, time and patience, the strength to ask for help, a lot of brainstorming and a belief in yourself and your right to an education.*

In fact, all the qualities that you would want as an employed professional. Fundraising is the ideal training ground for marketing and using your abilities. It will expose you to experiences of disappointment and success and equip you to handle both. One day you will graduate from your course and look for work. All the skills you learn from fundraising will stand you in good stead – not to mention how impressed a potential employer will be by your resourcefulness in raising thousands of pounds, dollars, or euros. This guide describes some useful starting points for your fundraising, including examples of fundraising strategies, budgets, press releases and letters to funding bodies.

You may still have doubts. At first, I did. It seemed an immense task – who on earth would give me £40,000 to train? No one I know has money like that. Realistically, you won't get the whole sum from one individual. But hundreds of people and organisations will give you twenty here, five hundred there and altogether, this adds up.

At the start of my fundraising, I had £200 in the bank – a gift from my family. Three months later I had raised £16,000. I am glad I had to raise the money. Now I know how to approach funding bodies and charities, organise events, budget, put together press releases, résumés and legal appeals, where to look for financial support and how to ask for it in an efficient, professional way – none of which I had known anything about previously.

I finished my training in 2001 and now I work as a freelance artist in the field I trained for. I love my work, knowing how hard I have worked to get where I am. It is still warming to know that many people have helped me get here and considered my training a worthwhile investment. Many continue to advise and support me and I am sure that in my lifetime I will do the same for someone else. So don't feel bad about asking for help. One day you may be the one being asked.

Ask for help in the right way

Okay. Imagine you are a benefactor with £250 to give to one of the following individuals in need. Read their 'blurb'. Which would you decide to help?

Myra Needy

'I have decided to go to drama school and eventually got a place at the London Dramatic College. My parents can't afford to pay and if I don't raise £40,000 by September, I can't go. I can't get a grant because I've already done a degree course. This will ruin my ambitions for a career in acting. Please help me, I don't know who else will.'

Suzy Proactive

'Having auditioned for drama school, I am thrilled with my offer of a place on the three-year acting course at the London College of Dramatic Studies. Unfortunately, neither my family nor I can afford the tuition fees of £9,000 per annum and I am ineligible for a grant from my local education authority. I have opened an account for my training fund with £500 from my earnings as a Saturday shop assistant and put together a funding strategy and budget (enclosed), which details exactly how I will go about raising the rest of the money. As a benefactor you can help by donating £25 to my training fund. In return you will be invited to all college productions, named in all publicity as an official donor and receive a certificate and termly report on my progress at drama school.'

Personally, I choose the second! Why? Their situations are the same, but their tones are very different. The second has such a positive approach and people love positivity. They tend not to respond to 'victim of fate' appeals, which can sound like begging. They want to know exactly what is required, where the money will come from and go to, how you will use it, why you are in this predicament and what they will get in return. They want to see realistic goals, working strategies and budgets and your belief that it is possible. If you are convinced of your own abilities, you will have a certain positive energy that will rub off on others and convince them also. They want to see someone who is helping herself. Only then will they trust that they are spending their money or time wisely.

WRITE YOUR OWN BLURB

Now you have seen how and how not to do it, have a go at writing your own blurb.

The following questions need to be answered:

• **What course will you be on and where?**

• **Why are you having to fundraise?**

• **How will you begin your fundraising?**

• **What can someone do to help?**

Follow the model of 'Suzy Proactive' opposite and keep the tone positive. When you are happy with your blurb, keep it by the phone and use it as a script for potential donors. Learn it off by heart and use it whenever someone asks you what you're doing.

Now you've begun, let's be clear about how much it will actually cost to go and train.

Checklist

✔ **Have you been accepted onto your chosen course?**

✔ **Are you prepared to fight for your training?**

✔ **Have you thought about your general approach to fundraising?**

Chapter two

Know what you want

What do you want? A good training followed by a successful career. Your obstacle? Tens of thousands of pounds, dollars, or euros. But exactly how much *will* it cost? Your first step is to calculate exactly what you need and table it as a budget.

Break it down

Breaking down your costs is essential for the following reasons:

• Once you know your specific requirements you can start looking for potential sources of help.

• Sometimes money can be replaced with 'donations in kind', for example, free meals in the college canteen for three years. This could save you a few thousand pounds.

• Charitable foundations and trusts tend to give money for tuition fees or specific maintenance costs, not both.

• Faced with a figure like £40,000, what is your immediate reaction? What a huge amount. Faced with a figure of £400 per year to cover travel costs… what a reasonable amount.

And it's strange… there is great comfort in looking at a budget, realising that you need smaller chunks of income for various things. Suddenly, all those thousands don't seem so intimidating. So let's look at budgeting.

Your budget

Budgeting is an art in itself. For this you will need a calculator, plenty of paper and a head for figures. Don't have a head for figures? Don't panic – get a willing volunteer and use his – or her – head for figures. Do have a go first though because, provided you are organised, you should be able to follow my instructions for budgeting step-by-step. The calculator will do all of the hard stuff.

A budget is simply a breakdown of how much money you have coming in and how much going out. Everyone with a job, home, or family will have experienced the joys of budgeting at one time or another.

For extra help, check out the budgeting tool, free to download at www.degreesforfree.com.

How much do I need?

You need a certain amount of money to pay for your education (tuition fees) and another amount to pay for your living costs (maintenance). Split these into two separate categories, because charities and patrons prefer to give money for one or the other.

Tuition fees

Call the university. The tuition costs should be listed in their prospectus, viewbook or application pack. If you do not have a definite offer of a place, find out the different tuition costs for each school to which you are applying and use the highest figure for your budget. Be specific; it is not enough to say 'approximately £9,000 per year'. Find out the different universities' policies on collecting tuition fees. How much of a deposit – if any – do they require? Are fees payable in advance, each term, or in annual instalments? Can you start each term or semester and pay as you go?

The deposit is your initial concern. If you were offered a place tomorrow, how would you find the money for it? Can anyone lend or give it to you? Do you have any savings? Can you get a loan? What happens if you are offered a place but want to wait to see if you get into somewhere else? In this case, will you get a refund?

For the purposes of this example, let us say your tuition fees are £9,500 per academic year.

Maintenance costs

Your maintenance costs include: room and board, utility bills (e.g. gas and electricity), local taxes, food, travel, books and equipment. It is helpful to work out their weekly cost first.

Find out how much you can expect to pay for housing. Check out your college's website or call them. Does your college provide cheap housing? If you have to rent privately, the adverts in the back of a local newspaper will help you to estimate average costs. Try also to get an estimate of how much local taxes are too. Do students get any kind of discount?

Base your gas, electricity and water figures on your household at the moment, or call the utility companies in the area where you wish to live. Find out if there are any special discounts or rates for students.

Your food costs should be based on what you eat now. Bear in mind that your food budget should consist of the food you need, not the food you'd have in your dream fridge – so wipe the ice cream and caviar off the list now. Training on a full-time course can be very physically demanding, so you will need plenty of nutritious, high-energy foods – particularly fresh fruit and vegetables and anything high in complex carbohydrates, such as rice or pasta. If necessary, contact your doctor who will be able to advise you further. And if you've never done the grocery shopping in your life, now is the time to start. Head for your local supermarket and check out the prices of all the products you would buy in a week. Don't forget household essentials like cleaning products and bathroom goods. You might also want to investigate the prices of the supermarkets in the area where you intend to live. I found that even the cheapest supermarkets in London were more expensive than the luxury supermarkets in my home town, and this added at least ten percent onto my estimated shopping budget.

Travel expenses are the costs incurred travelling between your home and the school. Does this involve train fares or buses? How much will a travel pass save you? Will you be travelling at peak or off-peak times?

Ring your college or university to find out their requirements for books and equipment. There is usually a list of books they will want you to read and perhaps specialised equipment – for example, a performing arts course may require you to provide dance shoes. Must you have the equipment before you begin?

To give you a rough guide, this total cost per week should be approximately the same as the weekly expenditure of any student or person on state benefit. If it is much higher, go back through your figures and ask yourself if you really need everything. It is highly unlikely that anyone will fund a luxurious budget. Yes, we all like going to clubs, buying new clothes and purchasing treats from the deli counter, but you'll have to get a part-time job if you have expensive tastes.

Be minimal but realistic

Many top educational courses are based in big cities like New York or London – the most expensive places to live, full stop.

For this example, I have listed some typical annual costs on page 10. These are your target figures for the purposes of fundraising. Check and double-check to ensure accuracy because trusts and businesses will reject your applications if your figures do not add up.

Give yourself a major pat on the back for having worked out your budget, which is no mean feat. Yes, £17,400 is more than some people's annual wage, but don't be put off. Figures out of the way, the creativity starts here – how you will go about raising this staggering sum.

Room (£75 per week x 52)	£3,900
Water (per year)	£150
Electricity (£125 quarterly x 4)	£500
Gas (£50 quarterly x 4)	£200
Food (£20 per week x 52)	£1,040
Books (per year)	£100
Equipment (per year)	£150
Travel costs (£30 per week x 52)	£1,560
Other local taxes (per year)	£300

TOTAL MAINTENANCE PER ANNUM £7,900

Divided by 52 gives a weekly living cost of £151.92

Now you should add the tuition costs and maintenance together:

£9,500 + £7,900 = £17,400

So your TOTAL ANNUAL EXPENDITURE will be £17,400

£17,400 x 3 (the number of years of your course) = £52,200

So the OVERALL COST of your attendance is £52,200

How much will I raise?

There are as many potential sources of income as your imagination will allow. However, I have broken them down into recognisable categories: grants, family support, charitable trusts and foundations, business support, patronage, college bursaries, personal income and fundraising events.

Grants and other financial support

Grants are sums of money given as a gift or granted without any expected repayment. Get in touch with your college or local education authority to find out about these and any other financial support for students. Their phone numbers will be listed in the telephone directory or on the internet.

Each course and school will be different depending on the type of course – is it a degree or a diploma? Are their grants mandatory (meaning everybody is entitled to the money) or discretionary (meaning it is up to the authority)? Do you have to audition, be interviewed, or compete against other students for the money? How much can you expect to receive and does it depend on your family income? If you are an older student are you assessed differently? Have you studied for a previous degree and does this affect the support they can offer? Find out if you are able to apply for any grants before you have the definite offer of a place. Unless you automatically qualify for a grant, *do not* include it in your income.

Family support

Will your family be able to help financially? Perhaps someone will lend you some money, although do not confuse getting into debt with raising money. You will not need to take out a loan if your fundraising is effective.

Personal

Do you have any income or savings? If you have a job, how much can you save from your employment before you go away to study? If you have children or a disability, can you claim any social security benefits while you are studying?

You shouldn't include any money you expect to earn from taking a part-time job while studying. Some courses require you to attend for forty hours per week, with extra evening and weekend commitments and homework. And what about when you have to prepare your dissertation and you can't afford the time to work? *Aim to raise enough money to live on without the need for a part-time job.* This is a last resort or an option if you want to supplement your income. Wait and see how arduous you find the course before you make that decision.

Charitable trusts and foundations

You can also apply to a trust or foundation, for help with the cost of your education. This particular source of income needs a great deal of research and time – I will go into further details later. In general, if you are in financial difficulty you apply to a trust for a fixed sum of money. Your case will be presented, on your behalf, to a board of trustees who will assess you against other applicants and the trust's individual criteria for support. They will then contact you with their decision – if positive, this will usually be in the form of a cheque. The applications are a lengthy process but in my experience very worthwhile – more than half of my annual income as a student came from trusts.

Business sponsorship

This will involve a similar amount of research and invested time but is a two-way partnership, not a gift. Based on your approach and the strength of your personal marketing skills, a company may decide to sponsor you. In return you will raise their profile with your well-structured campaign, keep them informed of your progress, invite them to your college productions and give them as much publicity as possible. Sometimes a company may agree to sponsor you provided you commit to working for them for a length of time when you graduate. All of these options should be investigated and you can find more information on this in chapter six.

Patronage

This is similar to business sponsorship but comes from an individual rather than a company. A patron does not expect any return from his or her donation.

Bursaries

College bursaries may be available to students in financial difficulty. Most large schools have a financial aid department that can help with hardship funds or competitive scholarships – contact your school for more information.

Events

These are the most active ways you can raise your money. The more events you organise thoroughly, the more money you will raise – it's as simple as that. But, they can fail if they are not planned carefully, *see* chapter eight to find out how to make sure your event is a huge success.

Your income from the above sources can only be predicted and depends very much on how much time you have to spend fundraising. Events need a great deal of effort and you may decide that your time is better spent working in a full-time job and saving hard right up to your first term. I opted successfully for a mixture of the two. Even with known prospects and previous donors, professional fundraisers expect a positive response rate of around ten percent – so for every hundred letters you write you might receive ten favourable replies. When writing to people they don't know it's likely to be less than one per cent. These are only averages. I wrote two hundred letters to national companies after fifty to sixty hours of research, preparation and letter writing. I received a hundred and ninety-nine refusals. Only one reply was favourable. Was it worth all that work, you ask? Yes – it was a contribution of £3,000 towards my training.

Work hard, work in detail and work to targets

Set your own targets for each of the categories in the above headings.

For my example budget, I aim to raise the following per academic year:

Business sponsorship	£2,000
Patronage	£2,000
Family support	£1,500
Personal income	£2,000
College bursaries	£2,900
Fundraising events	£3,000
Grants from charitable foundations and trusts	£4,000
PROJECTED ANNUAL INCOME	£17,400

You will have noticed two things. Firstly, I have not included grants from a local authority in my income breakdown, because there is no guarantee that it will be available. Secondly, the figures for my annual income and expenditure are identical: they match up. The books must balance.

Do not be disillusioned – there is no easy or set way to raise money as an individual in need. However, you now have realistic figures to work from and clear goals. At this point you need to think about your strategy.

Checklist

✔ **Have you paid your deposit?**

✔ **Do you know the exact amount of your tuition fees?**

✔ **Have you calculated your maintenance costs?**

✔ **Have you budgeted for other educational expenses, such as library fees, books and specialist equipment?**

✔ Have you drafted your 'expenditure' budget?

✔ Have you drafted your 'income' budget?

✔ Have you set yourself targets for each potential
source of income?

Chapter three

The strategy

Now all the figures are ready, it is time to create a strategy: a plan of action.

You will need a document that outlines your plan and schedule.

The deciding factor

Time: how much do you have before you start your course and how much can you put into fundraising? Organising one event will take relatively little time compared to sending out five hundred letters, but you may attract more sponsorship from the letters. The earlier you apply to a school, the earlier you will usually know if you have a place. But don't despair – it's never too late. I obtained my place in June and before September I had raised everything I needed for my first year.

Resources could be an obstacle

Or I should say lack of resources. I saved a great deal of time, as well as being able to present my sponsors with a well-designed and printed pack, using a PC, printer and photocopier. Are you computer literate? Do you have access to a computer? The postage costs of a mail shot can prove very expensive, not to mention buying stationery. If you intend to send out sponsorship packs and letters, my advice is to find an organisation that will donate the use of a PC and office equipment as their contribution to your fundraising efforts. You may have contacts through a family member's place of work, a relative with a small business, or a helpful local youth club. I was a member of a youth theatre before my training and the Belgrade Theatre kindly let me use their office facilities during my summer fundraising. Without something along these lines, you will incur pretty hefty administration costs yourself.

Your resources must also include a telephone and a place of research – I used my local library and the internet. Count the friends who will help you as your resources, too. If you are a member of a group or society, don't be afraid to ask for their help.

An essential

Communication is vital and must be clear. Learn to like using the telephone and meeting people. A friendly, personal approach will usually be met warmly, unlike a written demand in the post. You can help yourself by using scripts when telephoning, or by spending ten minutes thinking about what you want to say before you meet someone. It will help if you have some office experience, but there is a chapter on using the telephone and business letters later in this guide.

Another essential

Research will make or break your campaign. Sending out two hundred letters randomly is a complete waste of time and money and will simply irritate people, which may make them less receptive to other approaches. Sending out two hundred letters to the correct person at targeted companies takes a lot of research but will be far more effective. Be prepared to spend a good few hours writing down names and addresses from the internet, or from directories in your library. I recommend investing in a bumper pad, a pack of pens and a large flask of coffee.

A third essential

Preparation: the more you can plan in advance, the better. Giving yourself one week to organise a cabaret night is unrealistic; plan it eight weeks ahead and you will have covered most options and will have had time to sell most, if not all, of the tickets.

Attention seeking

Not always a bad thing – publicity is the best way of bringing your appeal to local attention. A good press article can advertise your events and turn your campaign into a recognised venture and may even attract a few donors. People will talk about you and it will demonstrate how committed you are. You can appeal for all sorts of things: good donations for car boot sales, attendance at your five-a-side match, acts for your cabaret night, etc. Chapter seven deals with these issues in greater detail and you can find a sample press release in appendix II and also online at www.degreesforfree.com.

Your ideas

It's time to brainstorm the ideas that come under your control. Take a piece of paper and write down all of the ideas you can possibly think of that could help you raise money. Get friends or family to help: two brains are better than one! Don't worry about organising it. We'll do that later.

Now organise your ideas into fundraising categories, see facing page.

You now have a list that looks like this:

PEOPLE TO WRITE TO:
Relatives, friends, work colleagues, ex-employers, big businesses, small businesses, Members of Parliament or Senators, peers, local charities, national charities, tycoons, media icons, clubs and social groups, former students of college, councillors.

ONE-OFF EVENTS:
Marathons, auctions, sports matches, exhibitions, fashion shows, karaokes, pub quiz, cabaret night, treasure hunt, poetry evening, barbecue, disco or club night, parachute jump, sponsored swim, blind date, jail break, competition, yard sale.

**Call Sian's dad and see if we can use his pub to host event.

**Can we use the hall in the temple? Ask Herveer.

REGULAR INCOME:
Wages, evening work, work from home, babysitting, selling t-shirts, organising drama workshops.

**Target: make £60 a week.

PUBLICITY:
Journalists, local newspapers, local radio stations, local TV companies, national press, hospital radio, local newsletters, circulars at work, school notice board, cable channels, shop windows, billboards, breakfast TV shows, publicity stunt in city precinct, flyers and posters.

GRANTS I ALREADY KNOW ABOUT:
Local education authority.

**Research more online and in library.

HOW MUCH CAN YOU RAISE?

Many of your applications for help will go to charities, businesses and grant-making organisations. You will be able to influence but not control the decision they make. Start by brainstorming the areas of fundraising you do have control over.

• Set a realistic weekly target to save money from your job.

• Call all of your family and friends. If you cannot ask them for money, ask for help in kind, or even time. If your dad's friend lets you use his office for all of your stationery and photocopying, great! Will your aunt organise a cake sale to raise money for you? Would your football team bathe in baked beans for you?

• What kinds of fundraising events and sponsorship schemes can you dream up? The more original the better. Normally, the more fun people have, the more money they are prepared to give.

• List all the suitable spaces you have connections with for events, like community centres, pubs, church groups, etc. Book the date for your karaoke night now to give you time to organise it. This will also give you a deadline to work to.

• Publicity can increase the profile of your campaign and help you to raise more money. How can you let the maximum number of people know about your campaign?

• Which grants that you already know about can you apply for right now?

Set yourself an achievable target for each event you hold and remember you can hold raffles and other pay-to-play games at each event to raise even more cash.

The plan of action

In order to organise your different targets and fundraising sources it is useful to draw up a targeted schedule of how much time you have and when events will take place. You can then begin to plan with deadlines and enough notice to co-ordinate events. Here is a sample schedule:

May 1st   Place on three-year course confirmed.

May 2nd   Apply for grants.

May 10th   Write to charities and businesses.

May 15th   First yard sale – target £150.

June 1st   Local media attention.

June 5th   Write to local MP, or Senator.

July 1st   Sponsored event – target £1,000.

July 5th   Write to individuals.

July 15th   Second yard sale – target £150.

Aug 1st   Entertainment night – target £350.

Aug 15th   Third yard sale – target £150.

Aug 30th   Perform show – target £500.

Sept 5th   Barbecue and fireworks party – target £300.

Sept 15th   Final yard sale – target £150.

Sept 18th   Quiz night – target £250.

Sept 20th   Prepare for move to college town.

Sept 25th   Term at school begins!

These are the bare bones of your plan. Apply to the largest grant-making organisation first. If you are awarded a grant this will reduce your fundraising target massively. Many foundations need to know if you have been accepted for any

SO WHAT'S YOUR STRATEGY?

Create a strategy document, outlining your plan of action and schedule. It needn't run to pages and pages and will come in handy for charities, businesses and your education authority's appeals committee, if need be. Here is part of one:

'**Businesses**. I will be writing to over two hundred businesses in order to attract sponsorship. In return for regular donations they will receive a certificate, accreditation in my publicity, invitations to college productions and a termly update on my progress. I intend to raise £2,000 from business sponsorship.'

'**Events**. I will be holding several fundraising events from which I hope to raise £3,000. These include yard sales, a karaoke night, a performance of scenes from Shakespeare, raffles and a sponsored swim. My schedule gives the dates on which these events are to take place.'

other grants before they will consider your application to avoid double-funding. Next apply to smaller trusts, then businesses and finally individuals. The order is based on the number of people who make decisions. Trustees of foundations meet infrequently, a submission to a business may have to go before a board of directors, whereas individuals can make their decision more or less straight away.

The next step

Now pencil in your events. Anything that will be ticketed or requires detailed preparation should be placed well into the future – ideally you'll have time to sell out. Hold fire on contacting local journalists until you have had some response from grant-making organisations and know the dates of your fundraising events in order to publicise them. Targets are difficult to set but should be realistic, according to your entry charges and predicted number of participants. If you are feeling in need of encouragement – and everyone does at some point – set your targets slightly on the low side rather than too high. Anything above your target will exceed your expectations instead of failing them. However, if you're feeling confident, or lucky, a high target will spur you on. If you aim for a hundred pounds rather than, say, fifty but only raise seventy-five, remember a seventy-five-pound failure is always better than a fifty-pound success.

Now you can begin your preparation.

Checklist

✔ **Have you managed to obtain the use of a PC?**

✔ **Have you thought about stationery, telephone and postage costs?**

✔ **Have you brainstormed the fundraising possibilities?**

✔ **Have you structured your ideas into a schedule with realistic fundraising targets?**

✔ **Have you created a strategy outlining your plan of action?**

Chapter four

Student grants and appeals

This chapter is primarily for students who are entitled to claim some money from the local authorities or the government towards the cost of their education. This applies to most prospective students in the UK, Canada, Australia, New Zealand and South Africa. But wherever you live in the world, if you are applying for any kind of grant or having to follow an appeal against a funding decision made against you, this chapter will be of help.

Essentially, apply for a grant as soon as possible. Read the application pack carefully so that you can calculate how much you may be entitled to. Sometimes grants are income dependent so you will need to collect either your own tax returns and wage slips, or those of your parents if you are a minor.

If you have children, adult dependants, or a disability you may be eligible for extra financial help. It is also worth checking whether there are any regional awards given in the area in which you live. There may be slightly different criteria for postgraduate students. Contact the grant-making authority in each case for more details.

Discretionary grants

If there are no automatic grants, there may be discretionary grants available. A discretionary grant means that the authority can choose whether or not it is awarded. Each grant-making authority has its own rules on making awards to students.

If you are applying for a discretionary grant, you should gain as much information about the procedure as possible from the senior officer at the grant-making authority. Find out the kinds of courses and circumstances under which previous discretionary grants have been made, what criteria have to be fulfilled, how long you can expect to wait for a decision and who will be making that decision. Then establish if there is anything you can do to support your application.

If you are refused a discretionary grant, you sometimes have the right to a written appeal. Ask the local authority for a copy of its appeals procedure. *You must appeal.* Some authorities seem to flatly refuse all discretionary grants immediately, perhaps knowing that many students will be put off by the appeals procedure. Don't be. Like any legal appeal, a panel will be called to examine all submissions. They will consider the appeal and take a vote.

Students are usually notified in writing of the decision on their discretionary grant together with the reasons why it was accepted or rejected. Most applications in the UK for discretionary grants from local education authorities are turned down for the reason that 'they are not exceptional enough'. Don't take this too personally, of course you are exceptional. Try telling anyone who has battled with over a thousand other students for one of thirty places that they are 'not an exceptional case'. Call the senior officer back to find out what they *would* class as 'an exceptional case'. Even if you get no joy, you have a fantastic story for the press, and your anger will only help fuel your fighting spirit.

Appealing against decisions

If you are appealing in respect of a student grant you must put together a well-documented, well-presented and watertight case. Your aim is to cover every possible criterion, leaving no gaps and to make it as difficult as possible for the appeals panel to turn you down. You may not have a great deal of time – I was given two weeks from the date of my refusal letter in which to appeal, so be prepared.

It is tempting to go for media attention at this stage. You will no doubt be disappointed to be refused a grant and the local press love a headline like 'City Authorities Refuse Young Star'. My suggestion is to hold fire. Although you may attract public sympathy, it will not strengthen your case in the eyes of the appeals panel. However, it may be beneficial to write to your local government representatives. Their investigation into your case may be of help.

The appeal form will allow you space to give your reasons for appealing against the decision. Acceptable reasons include adverse family circumstances, ill health or disability, domestic or financial hardship and the elusive 'exceptional case' clause. You must also prove that your course of study is of a higher level to that you might previously have attained, so if you are a postgraduate student you need to check the appeal criteria carefully to find out if this will affect you.

Assuming you are appealing because your family does not earn enough to pay your tuition fees, not because you have suffered previous ill health or are registered disabled, you will have to prove that you are 'an exceptional case'. In my opinion, having been through a gruelling selection process in order to gain a place at a highly respected college is exceptional in itself, but the appeals committee may not take this view.

The appeals committee will be asking the following questions.

Why do you need to train here instead of anywhere else?
It might be that you are undertaking a purely vocational course and will be taught by professionals, not lecturers. Examples of such a course might be ballet, acting, or music. Your work is showcased with a view to obtaining an agent and you are being trained purely to be a professional, *not* an academic or teacher. Perhaps you have been offered a place at a top college and you left school as top of your year. Surely exceptional talent should receive the very best education?

How will you use your training?

Give a thorough plan of how you intend to approach your career after graduation, including what you will do to seek work. Link the skills you will gain at your school to your future employment; for example, three years of voice classes means that you will be able to work in radio or as a voice-over artist. You should aim to make the appeals panel see their grant as an investment in the future of your chosen profession. It may be a good idea to think of some way of linking your training back to your local community. Would you be able to return to your home city after graduation and offer free lectures to undergraduates? The panel may be persuaded to vote for you if they see your award as benefiting the local area.

What is your track record?

Enclose a résumé, showing all related work experience. For example, if you were a member of a local dance school, list all of the productions you have been in.

Describe how you came to apply for and be accepted at your place of education.

Include written references from reputable sources: previous teachers, the principal of your school, youth leaders, anyone you have worked with. Your referees should not only describe how talented you are, but why this kind of learning is essential for your career and, financially, how much of a setback it would be if your appeal was refused.

Why can't you pay for the fees yourself?

Give them a breakdown of your (and your parents', if necessary) weekly income and expenditure, including official proof such as wage slips, bank statements, social security letters and tax returns.

How will you raise the rest of your tuition or maintenance costs?

You already have a fundraising strategy and budget. Include a concise, clearly typed copy.

Only submit your appeal when you are satisfied that you have covered all criteria, with proof. Then it's back to the waiting game while other people make the decisions. The excitement of going off to train may seem like it's still a long way off. The best thing you can do is to forget about the grant. Even if you get a refusal, there are other ways to raise that money. I did it – and so can you.

What if the appeal is rejected?

If your appeal if refused you have several courses of action. You may be able to appeal again, or complain at a higher level. The letter of refusal should outline what you should do if you wish to take things further.

In the UK, you can complain to the Commission for Local Administration (the ombudsman) if you feel that your appeal case suffered through maladministration, which you may have to prove. Maladministration means that the appeals committee did not follow their own guidelines.

In every democracy you will be able to take your right to appeal to the very highest legal levels with the aid of a solicitor or attorney.

My advice is: accept the decision and channel your energies into fundraising. You will be much more likely to get help if you can show that you tried, but your appeal was unsuccessful, so make sure you keep a copy of your appeal and the decision letter as proof. This is a good time to contact local journalists and highlight not only your case, but also the plight of students like yourself in general.

Most appeals are refused for one simple reason – grant-making authorities rarely have big budgets and funding you means that they would have to fund every similar student and, therefore, be forced to change their policy. This is an unfortunate reality of the world we live in now. In an ideal world, everyone would be able to follow the path of education they choose, regardless of financial background.

Anyway, best of luck with your appeal. If nothing else, you have done all you could to try and raise your money. You have also had excellent practice in proving your right to a training that you will need later. And, who knows, perhaps because of you, the authorities will change their policy on funding certain kinds of training.

Checklist

✔ **Have you received all of the information and the application for each grant?**

✔ **Have you spoken to your local authority about your chosen training course and the help available in your situation?**

✔ **Do you need to apply for a discretionary award?**

✔ **Can you provide written references from your mentors?**

✔ **Can you prove why you should be entitled to the money?**

Chapter five

Charitable foundations, trusts and grant-making organisations

Charitable foundations, trusts and grant-making organisations exist to help individuals and organisations in need. There are thousands of such bodies all over the world, varying in size from well-known organisations, such as the Ford Foundation, to small family trusts. Of the 10,000 endowed grant-making foundations in the UK, only a couple of hundred or so have annual incomes of over a million pounds. Each foundation has its own specific criteria and guidelines.

There are about 4,000 charitable foundations in the UK that give to individuals and a fairly large proportion of these *only* give to individuals. Of those that give for education, significantly fewer are interested in postgraduate education; many will not consider people who have already studied at undergraduate level and there are a whole host of restrictions on who is eligible for financial help. Most foundations receive hundreds of applications every year, which are assessed by a monitoring group, usually the trustees, who may not meet more than four times a year.

It might sound daunting and pointless to apply, but there are foundations that will help you. With careful research and planning you can highlight those grant-making bodies to which you are eligible and submit a strong application based on your needs.

Where will I find the information?

Research is essential. You will waste time and paper in applying haphazardly to a lot of random foundations. Firstly, visit your local library, careers office, or college financial aid office and check what's out there. Some guides are listed in appendix I.

In the UK, the Educational Grants Advisory Service (EGAS) is a helpful service that may be able to help you. It is an advisory service set up by Family Action, specialising in assisting students seeking help from educational trusts. In addition to information on Family Action's own educational grant-making trusts, EGAS has all up-to-date information on loans, grants and benefits. If you fill in their application form, they will carry out a free search from their database and send you a list of grant-making foundations. To maximise the number of charitable foundations EGAS can put you in contact with, I recommend that when you fill in their application form you only ask for a few hundred pounds; very few of the foundations on the EGAS database have the resources to fund you into the thousands. EGAS is a great source of help for any student; you should contact the coordinator of educational grants and advice at the address listed for Family Action in appendix I.

Scholarships may be available directly from your school. Most schools and colleges have financial aid departments that can help with hardship. A scholarship is a financial award for an individual student and your eligibility is based on criteria that reflect the values of its original benefactor. Often these are competitive and you will be amongst many students trying to get hold of a limited resource of money. Contact the school for more information and ask about the scholarships they offer. Sometimes they are referred to as bursaries.

You can also research scholarships at www.scholarship-search.org.uk, where you will find information on scholarships, bursaries and awards.

I have my list of foundations – what next?

Call or write to them and find out how you should go about making an application. Check their criteria and contact details; find out how often awards are made. It is also worthwhile investigating the size of their average grant and the number of awards made. Request an application form if they have one. You may have to send a small cheque to cover their administration costs for postage, or enclose a stamped, self-addressed envelope.

Don't, under any circumstances, send a standard letter. By this I mean photocopying a hundred letters and addressing them all 'Dear Sir/Madam'. Foundations – in fact, just about everyone – hate this kind of generalised approach and, while it may save you time, your letters will end up in the bin. Always address your application to a specific named person. If you really cannot find out whom you should write to, address your application to 'The Grants Administrator'. You shouldn't apply to foundations until you have the definite offer of a place at a school. Otherwise you may have a few cheques to tear up and apology letters to send.

At this point I suggest you make a database of your information on foundations. Sometimes a foundation will not reply for six months and you will want to keep track of which applications are still outstanding.

How do I know what the foundation wants?

When a charitable foundation or trust is set up, the founder creates a trust deed that describes which particular charitable purposes the money should be used on. It is the trustees' job to ensure that the money is spent according to the trust deed. Read the awards criteria very carefully to see if you fit the bill. Some foundations have quite generalised guidelines, some very specific. If you are unsure if you are suitable, it will do no harm to give them a call. If you are limited for time and resources, I recommend you only apply to trusts within whose guidelines you are sure you definitely fit. Here are two examples of foundations to which a drama student may be eligible.

Dr Rathbone Foundation

The Foundation was set up in 1926 at the bequest of James D Rathbone in order to help arts organisations and artists. The trustees meet in March and September and past awards have been of between £50 and £15,000.

The Aldgate Trust

In 1999, the Trust declared performing arts students as its area of interest. The deadline for returning completed application forms is June 30th and the criteria are as follows:

i) Students must be under 25 years of age and living in Aldgate.

ii) Students in receipt of major grants or awards are ineligible.

iii) Students must be able to prove that they are in financial hardship and their application must be supported by two written references.

iv) Awards will only be made for books, equipment, study materials, or travel costs of between £50 and £250. Please note that awards will not be given for tuition fees or maintenance costs.

v) The trustees will not consider students with a shortfall of more than £1,500.

It is very clear what the Aldgate Trust is looking for, the Rathbone Foundation much less so. Once you have as much information as you can find, tailor each application to suit each organisation. Please note that I am referring to the *presentation* of your details – never lie about your situation. Foundations invariably follow up on their award recipients and obtaining money under false pretences is a criminal offence.

If you have already had to appeal a grant-making authority's decision, you will find applying to charitable foundations a very similar process.

What should I mention in my application?

Whether you have to fill in an application form or not, the foundation's trustees will want to know the same information. Here is a list of details commonly asked for by foundations and a guide to answering their questions.

For what purpose do you require help?

In other words, 'How much do you want and why?' Read the organisation's guidelines. If they will only give travel grants then you need 'assistance with travel costs whilst attending X course'. The same applies to any restrictions on how awards are to be used. If there are no restrictions then you need 'assistance with tuition fees and maintenance costs for X course at Y college'.

How much should you ask for?

If awards are limited to £250, don't ask for any more because you won't get it. If awards are unlimited, use your judgement. Check the foundation's record of grant-making to see how much has been given in the past. Some prefer to give sizeable amounts to only a few individuals; others donate smaller amounts to many people. If a foundation wants to help you, it will – even if it can only give half of the amount you asked for. From your budget the trustees will see that you are very realistic about the amount of money you need to raise.

What is your past record of achievement?

Your 'past record of achievement' will include your academic qualifications, your employment history and participation in your chosen field of study up until the present. Of course you will want to list any competitions you have entered and prizes you may have won, relevant courses or skills training you have completed (for example, dancing examinations), extra-curricular activities and any relevant projects you have been involved with. Were you top of your class or valedictorian? Were you a straight A-grade student? Keep it brief and relevant – they do not need to know that the jokes you put in the school play in December 2003 went down well with the teaching staff.

Obtain two written references from your past tutors or youth leaders to support your record of involvement, even if the foundation has not specifically requested them. Include copies of one or two press articles, if they demonstrate your ability and your predicament.

What is your financial situation?

Give details of your current income and expenditure, with wage slips and tax returns as proof. Include details and proof of your parents' financial situation, as it is highly likely that the foundation will want to know why your family cannot cover the shortfall. If you have any dependants, or your parents have any other children, give their ages and state of dependency, for example, 'I have two sisters, aged 12 and 17, who are both still at school and living at home'. Don't be embarrassed to mention any other factors of financial hardship within your family. It will support your case.

You should also tell them about the response from major grant-making authorities. If you were turned down, provide a copy of the decision letter.

Remember to just present facts. If you read your application and find a section that seems to plead or complain, rewrite it. Keep it based on truths you can provide evidence for.

Show how you intend to raise the rest of your money

When you send your application, you should include your budget and up-to-date information on any monies you have already raised, together with a list of all other foundations and trusts you have applied to. Provide a copy of your fundraising strategy as well, so that they can see how you will raise the rest of the money.

Your career intentions

Tell them how you will benefit from training and how you intend to use this training for your future career. It is fair to say that no other form of training will prepare you for a career. Tell them how you intend to find work after graduation.

Further relevant information

Give them an idea of how important it is for you to raise the money for your intended course. If you cannot raise the necessary funding you will be unable to pursue this incredible opportunity. Tell them why your school is unable to cover the cost of your fees. Most colleges are registered charities and as such are able to offer only limited support in the form of bursaries and scholarships.

One vital thing – don't waffle. It makes for a boring read. If you have answered the above questions you should have given the trustees all the information they need to know. If they require any further details, they will contact you. It is a good idea to show your applications to a colleague for feedback.

Finally, check your application for spelling mistakes and take a photocopy. You should include a covering letter with the application and a stamped self-addressed envelope for the foundation's reply. The covering letter need not say very much, something along the lines of:

'Please find enclosed my completed application form and supporting documents. If you need any further information, please contact me at the above address. Thank you for your attention.'

Now stick it in an envelope and mail it. You may not receive a reply, not because your case is unworthy but simply because foundations are swamped with applications and most have very limited funds available. Never bank on receiving money from a foundation. But if you have an exceptionally strong case, you will stand in good stead for favourable consideration. Carry on with the rest of your fundraising, forget about your application, and at some point you may be pleasantly surprised.

Keep all the replies you receive, whether favourable or not. Your college will be more inclined to give you financial aid once they have a huge pile of your 'no' letters and can see how hard you've worked to raise funds. If you discover a foundation that gives grants to organisations or registered charities, pass their details to the bursar at your training centre who may apply for money directly.

Checklist

✔ **Application form (if required).**

✔ **Covering letter.**

✔ **Amount requested.**

✔ **Budget.**

✔ **Fundraising strategy document and schedule.**

✔ **Copy of letter confirming place at school or college.**

✔ **Copies of two references.**

✔ **Copy of the refusal of a grant from the local education authority.**

✔ Résumé.

✔ Tax returns and wage slips as proof of financial hardship.

✔ Educational background.

✔ Future career intentions.

✔ Background information on your family situation.

✔ Press cuttings (optional).

✔ Stamped, self-addressed envelope.

Chapter six

Sponsorship

Sponsorship is the hardest fundraising nut to crack. Each sponsorship approach must be individual, based on research and both thought out and targeted properly.

What is sponsorship?

The difference between sponsorship and charitable donations is that your sponsor will gain something in return. Therefore your request will be very different from asking a foundation or trust for money. When you apply to a charitable trust, you are asking for their help in your time of need; they exist to give money away, commercial organisations exist to make a profit for their shareholders. When you apply for sponsorship, you are offering a company an incredible opportunity. You are not asking them for money, you are asking them to make an investment that will yield them a clear level of commercial return. Because sponsorship is more like a partnership, your sponsor has a greater level of involvement with your cause.

Charitable foundations have very clear guidelines within which you must fall in order to be successful. While larger companies will have policies on support in the community and sponsorship, smaller local businesses may not. Your sponsorship approach must be seen as an exciting, worthwhile and professional opportunity. Your method of presentation is entirely up to you.

Why should a company sponsor me?

The company's products will receive a higher profile through your publicity. The company name will be linked to a good cause and they will have the chance to put something back into the community. They will receive your thanks. You will be able to advertise the company to a specific target audience.

A company's chief executive may agree to a sponsorship deal for many reasons. One is profile – he wants maximum exposure of his business. Another is vanity – he wants his business to look good. Finally there is whim – imagine a letter from a drama student landing on his desk after he enjoyed an entertaining evening at the theatre the previous night.

Sometimes sponsorship will lead to you being officially contracted to work for the company upon completion of your course. This tends to happen more in the fields of science and engineering but the options are worth investigating.

Your college will be able to help you. Check with the bursar, registrar, or financial aid department to find out if there is a policy on company giving. What can the college offer a sponsor? This might include acknowledging the company in the prospectus and programmes, complimentary tickets for student productions, a guided tour of facilities, or hosting an annual sponsors' dinner. Add whatever your college can offer into your sponsorship deal.

You should add a personal touch. No sponsor will expect you to graft endlessly, nor is it appropriate, but here are a few ideas for your own package:

• A specially designed certificate.

• A termly report on your progress.

• A personal invitation to your college productions or other open events.

• Photographs for the company's brochure.

• A photo opportunity with the local press.

• A half-day skills workshop with the company's employees.

• The company name and logo on your résumé.

Can you offer something different? The Central School of Ballet choreographed a dance dramatising the entire sponsorship process from the first phone call to the presentation meeting. Their sponsor agreed immediately. Something a little out of the ordinary will have added attraction and will whet the appetite of a potential sponsor.

How do I know what I want from my sponsor?

Quantify your need. How much money do you want to apply for? I suggest offering your potential sponsors a menu of options, for example, £2,000 to become your sole sponsor, £500 to become a joint sponsor and £100 as a one-off donation. Each option should offer the companies something different according to their level of support. You could link a certain industry with a certain part of your budget, for example, £500 for your annual travel fare from a 'travel sponsor', from among your local vehicle manufacturers or sales showrooms.

If you do find a sole sponsor, you must be given the total amount of business sponsorship you have targeted in your budget. You must also stick to your side of the bargain and not allow any other businesses to sponsor you.

If you decide to attract joint sponsors, make sure the companies are not in direct competition. Businesses want as much of the market as they can get – partly through profitability and partly through corporate identity and pride. If you are applying to several companies of a similar nature, wait for an answer from the first before you apply to the second – you don't want to suddenly find yourself with two rival businesses as joint sponsors and some explaining to do. Be aware of company values. A nuclear power plant and a mineral water producer may not wish to be named together as sponsors.

How do I find suitable companies?

Build a profile of your ideal sponsor. Are you looking for a locally based sponsor, a large national business, or an international company? You would assume that the bigger the company, the bigger their profits and the more money allocated for company giving, but it isn't always so – many of the largest companies keep profit for reinvestment in the company – and their shareholders. Also, be aware that most national companies have definite policies on sponsorship, and many will not support individuals. Smaller, local companies may have less money to give, but they will receive far fewer requests for sponsorship.

BRAINSTORM SPONSORS

• Using a telephone directory, make a list of all the businesses that have something in common with one particular area of need that you have. For example:

Food, cost per annum: £750
Local supermarkets, fruit and veg shop, organic grocers, the deli on the high street.

Travel, cost per annum: £1,500
Local bike shop, service stations, independent car dealers, bus company.

• Get their contact details and target them specifically for sponsorship to cover your costs in that specific area.

It is worthwhile investigating any national companies with headquarters in your area – see appendix I for suggested guidebooks. Make enquiries at local business networks, for instance Rotary Clubs – they may be able to give you more detailed information on local companies. Check recent news articles for details of companies who are expanding or opening central offices near you, or companies who could do with improving their image. Do not make judgements about types of local business. A builder's yard may be as interested in sponsorship as a firm of solicitors. You will find local businesses in directories such as the Yellow Pages (in the UK), your library, or on the internet.

Make the most of your own contacts. You'll most likely be surprised at how many you have. If you are currently employed, would your employer be interested in sponsoring you? Or maybe your parents' employers; who else do they know? Do you have any vague connection with any company? Is your friend's mother self-employed? Investigate all possible associations because it stands in your favour to have an existing link with a company.

How do I begin my approach?

The sponsorship process can be lengthy and it may take time to progress from your initial telephone call to finalising the deal. You must be patient and under no circumstances try to force a swift decision – if a company isn't interested, move on. They have lost a valuable sales opportunity and the chance to gain profile; you have lost nothing.

Stage one: telephone enquiry

Phone the company headquarters and ask to be put through to the department dealing with sponsorship or charitable enquiries. If the operator is unsure, ask for the department handling press enquiries. If this is a smaller company ask for the managing director. When you have been connected to the right department, find out the name and title of the person responsible for sponsorship and then ask to speak to him or her. When you have been put through make sure that he or she actually is responsible for sponsorship. Ask if she handles applications. If not, find out the name and address of the person who does. Find out if the company has a preferred area of need; or if there is there any information on the company's giving that could be sent to you.

Now you have a more complete profile of your company and know who to write to. Unless you fall outside of the company's guidelines on sponsorship, the next step is to make contact with more details.

Stage two: the draft letter

Introduce yourself in your letter. Explain that you are writing with an opportunity for sponsorship. List the sponsor's options, including the cost and length of sponsorship. Two or more years means that the sponsor's name will be strongly identified with your cause and means the organisation will receive 'repeat exposure' from your publicity. List specifically what will be received in return for sponsorship. It is worth briefly mentioning the history of your school or college and naming some famous ex-students – the sponsor will be reaching an exclusive audience. Explain your track record and successes. Demonstrate how hard you have worked to achieve your place and to raise the necessary funding. Describe your future career plans. If you intend to work locally, explain that you will be putting your skills back into the local community. List any other sponsors. Finally, tell the company to get in touch if they are interested. You can then arrange a meeting to discuss your sponsorship further.

The tone of your letter should be one of opportunity, future and quality. A sample letter is available in appendix II and also in a free downloadable format at www.degreesforfree.com. Include a copy of your college brochure and press cuttings, if you have them. You might choose to include a pamphlet all about yourself.

When the Yvonne Arnand Theatre (Guildford, UK) ran a sponsorship drive, they said in their letters that they would make a follow-up call after fourteen days to discuss sponsorship. They included a cut-off return slip for any company that didn't wish to be contacted by telephone and many of the returned 'no thanks' slips arrived with a cheque for a small donation.

You may decide to follow up your letter with a telephone call. When put through to the right person, ask if your information has been received. Say that you would very much like to arrange a meeting to discuss the potential for sponsorship. If the company is not interested, you will be told at this stage, you won't be waiting for a phone call and you can safely cross that particular company off your list. If the company agrees to a meeting the interest will be genuine and if you present your case well you should get your sponsorship.

Stage three: the meeting

Present yourself well – you are your product. Check the time of the meeting, the location and the names and roles of all present. If you intend to take someone along, inform the company of his or her name and position first. Try to keep numbers to a minimum; committees are renowned for delays. The more people, the more time it takes to reach a unanimous decision. Be punctual. Take any official publications from your college, any press cuttings about your cause and any further details about the sponsorship package. During the discussion, emphasise how much your work is worth supporting. Empathise with the company at all costs and play up the benefits for them – name-drop famous ex-students and any college links with their business. Let somebody take the minutes of the meeting. If this is somebody from the company, make sure they agree to forward the minutes onto you by email or post, so you have a record of the meeting.

You may need to negotiate some of the terms of the sponsorship and you should be prepared for this before the meeting. What is the minimum you can accept? If you are offered £1,000 instead of £2,000 will the company settle for being a joint sponsor, not sole sponsor? Which elements of the sponsorship plan are you prepared to be flexible with? What do you consider to be an appropriate level of 'interference' from your sponsor?

Leave them to consider your proposal. With any luck, you will shortly receive a positive reply, a cheque for the agreed amount and have successfully launched your sponsorship!

Stage four: first benefits

Concentrate on the immediate elements of your sponsorship package. Contact local journalists with a press release informing them of your sponsorship. Contact the bursar or registrar at your college to tell them about your sponsor. Put together your sponsor pack, which may include a certificate and photographs and must include a letter of thanks. Saying thank you is one of the most important things a fundraiser should do. Work as closely as possible with the company in order to give them the greatest amount of publicity possible.

Stage five: continuing the partnership

Keep your sponsor informed of your progress. Termly reports are ideal. Keep to the conditions of the sponsorship agreement at all costs. You should keep sponsors informed of any changes to your situation – sponsors don't like surprises. Review the sponsorship at intervals to discuss its progress and evaluate both parties' involvement.

Be warned – the following should be avoided:

• Do not corner the chief executive at a social function to talk about sponsorship.

• Do not send photocopied circulars – they will end up in the waste bin.

• Do not approach the same company twice.

• Do not send lavish leaflets. It will look like you have enough money already.

• Do not allow rival companies or companies whose interests clash to become joint sponsors.

• Do not use guilt trips.

• Do not make sponsorship the means to fill a gap in your budget; this is an investment opportunity.

Finally, good luck! Securing sponsorship is a major achievement for any fundraiser. It is hard work to investigate and design your sponsorship packages to each company's needs, but so worthwhile for the promise of a mutually beneficial partnership. It can be very rewarding to see your photograph used in a company brochure; rewarding too for the employees who read your progress report on the notice board. Sponsorship is not a quick or easy way to make money, but a long-term commitment and hopefully the start of an enjoyable and fruitful relationship.

Checklist

✔ **Have you decided what a potential sponsor will receive in return?**

✔ **Have you set differing levels of sponsorship?**

✔ **Have you researched both local and national companies?**

✔ **Have you investigated links through family and friends?**

✔ **Have you established each company's policy on sponsorship and found the right person to write to?**

✔ **Have you drafted your letter seeking sponsorship?**

Chapter seven

Raising your campaign profile

The more people know about your fundraising campaign, the better. Publicity in the media can be used to raise awareness about the plight of students, promote your fundraising events, get publicity for your sponsors and may even attract a few phone calls of support.

Don't plan on having just one article in the free weekly paper; you should take advantage of all the different media in your area for different elements of your campaign. To target your resources effectively, you need a good working knowledge about the local media, journalists, printers, photographers, etc. I recommend keeping a database of contact details: the dates you contacted them and the outcomes. This will help you to prioritise in the future, make sure you can deal with responses to publicity and identify how well you are getting your message across. Your fundraising will be ongoing and you will use these details in the future.

You should be clear of your objectives when planning your publicity and promotion: whom do you want to contact and what effect do you want to have? You will want local people to understand your achievement of a place at a school and the seriousness of your financial predicament. You will want them to empathise with you, talk about you, feel moved to help you. It is not only what you say but also how you say it, so you will need to think carefully about how you present your case. Here are several pointers for dealing with the media in general.

Adopt a positive tone

It is no good complaining about the fact that you can't afford to train. Don't try to play the sympathy card; if you seem downhearted no one will believe in your cause. You want to appear one hundred percent positive and sure that with hard work and support you will achieve your targets, complete your studies and go on to follow your chosen career. Explain how you will raise the money with your fundraising campaign. Appear proactive and people will rally; everyone likes to help people who help themselves.

Communicate more in less space

Be clear and direct. Don't waste words. Avoid the passive tone, 'It was decided that…', which sounds bureaucratic and detached. Clichés are clichés because they are overused – stay away from them. Jargon will make your case inaccessible to everyone.

Pictures speak volumes

A good quality photograph can say much more than the equivalent space filled with words. Poor quality photographs that do not illustrate your message are a waste of time and space. Most photographs in newspapers are close-ups or action photos, so bear this in mind if you intend to use photographs for publicity.

Stick to the facts

Do not make statements that are untrue. Do not make allegations or damaging comments about anyone's reputation unless you want a lawsuit for defamation of character. Generalised comments and innuendo can be defamatory as well as specific statements, so just present the facts of your case and leave your audience to make the judgements.

Ways to use the media

You can publicise your campaign through press releases, news features, interviews, publicity stunts, leaflets and newsletters. Here are a few examples of how the media might be used for a fundraising campaign:

Article in *Evening Telegraph*

Headlined 'Curtain Rises On Cash Struggle', this full-page article explained the situation of two drama students in the city, with a list of TV personalities who were ex-students at their school. It included 'tips for newcomers' from a well-known local actor. It also reported the launch of their fundraising campaigns and details of forthcoming events.

Musical revue in shopping centre

A half-hour medley of songs performed on a Saturday in the town centre publicised a forthcoming cabaret evening. It was repeated four times throughout the day and flyers were distributed to shoppers during the songs. Advanced tickets were sold at a discount.

Commercial radio interview

Themed ten-minute slot: 'I Want To Be An Actor'. An interview with a local DJ with a fundraising update and advice for young people interested in theatre, including a phone-in for questions. The local business sponsor was mentioned and their jingle was played.

Leaflet to attract sponsors

A5 flyers were left in a local Chamber of Commerce and business clubs, which described the exciting potential for sponsor and student and focused on the prestige of the drama school. They included photos of the student and a brief explanation of back ground, fundraising strategy and budget.

A well-written press release will lead to interviews and newspaper articles and can be sent to any media contact, for instance newspaper journalists, radio stations, television news companies. It should be typed in large, clear print and will answer the questions 'who, what, when, where and why?' in an economical style. Choose a dynamic, dramatic headline and try to link positives to negatives, for example, 'Amazing Young Medic Grapples With Funding Crisis'. If you want to promote your sponsor, ask them to provide a quote or link them to your quote if they don't mind. Keep to a single A4 sheet and put the words 'Press Release' in large print near the top. Address the press release to a named journalist or the news editor, including a contact name and telephone number at the end of it. Make sure you are available for comment and follow up the press release with a phone call. If you are sending photographs, send your press release and photograph to the pictures editor at your local newspaper.

A sample press release can be found in appendix II and also to download at www.degreesforfree.com.

Bear in mind that journalists are looking for dramatic news and may suggest that you link with an existing news feature or create an opportunity for one, called 'finding an angle' in the trade. It may be worthwhile to have a few suggestions ready when you make your follow-up phone calls. You could meet a retired professional or the director of a linked institution for a radio programme. You could be filmed helping out with a primary school class for local TV news.

Once you have begun your campaign, keep the journalists up to date on your progress and let them know any forthcoming events or crucial decisions – when your education authority appeal will be heard, for example.

Publicity is a powerful tool in supporting your achievements and with a considered approach you can reap the benefits.

CREATE YOUR OWN PRESS RELEASE

• Using a telephone directory or the internet, list all of the media contacts for newspapers, radio and TV you can find.

• Have a go at a dramatic headline – describe yourself in as positive a way as you can and make your situation sound as negative as possible.

• Ring the college to find out if they have any notable news. Are they celebrating an anniversary or building new premises? Who are their well-known ex-students?

• Has anyone in your area been to the same school? Would they comment? Has anyone else from your area been in a similar situation to you?

• Describe how rigorous the selection is for your college; say how many people apply each year and the number of places that are actually available. Describe the selection process, how long it took and what each stage involved.

• List your past achievements, membership of clubs, amateur groups – where people might have seen you before.

• Collect comments from reputable people who know your work – teachers, youth leaders, your local MP or councillor, the principal of your school.

• Be as imaginative as possible in describing how your training will benefit you and your future career plans. Aim high.

• Describe your fundraising campaign: targets, deadlines and immediate events. You might want to highlight the fact that thousands of other young people nationally are in a similar plight.

• Put all of the above together on a single sheet of A4 and remember to include how people can help you or find out more information.

Checklist

✔ Have you researched local media contacts, including TV, radio and newspapers?

✔ Have you listed all publicity stunts you could hold?

✔ Have you listed places to leave flyers where potential donors will see them?

✔ Have you written and sent a press release?

✔ Can you come up with suggestions that might help journalists to 'find an angle' on your story?

Chapter eight

Fundraising and sponsored events

There is only one limit to the number of ways to host one-off
events and that is your imagination and even though an
outdoor fete, say, and a sponsored parachute jump are
completely different, they both share methods of
organisation. When choosing a theme, opt for something that
you will enjoy – why shouldn't you have a bit of fun raising
money? Secondly, don't be too ambitious. People will be glad
to join in without expecting something on the scale of Live 8.
Thirdly, consider the type of people you want to attend. A
promotional garage music night may be less popular with the
over-fifties; the eighteen-to-thirty age group may not be
enthusiastic about buying tickets for ballroom dancing.
Choose and market events relevant to the groups of people
you know best.

Decide if you want to organise something fairly low key to see
how much you make, or take on a major event with the
prospect of major results. Plan well in advance to obtain all
necessary permissions, sort out your requirements for the
evening and to drum up a good crowd. Keep your costs as
low as possible – the point is for you to raise money, not
spend it. If your event is likely to be costly, you could try to
obtain sponsorship from a local company – a local supplier of
mineral water may sponsor a charity fun-run, for example.

Make sure that your event doesn't clash with any other
events, like the World Cup Final, or the Super Bowl, for
instance. You should also check for any more local events

that could attract your audience. The weather will be a consideration for an outdoor activity.

Some examples of fundraising activities:

• Car washing.

• Live music night.

• Ticketed karaoke evening.

• Swim-a-thon.

• Charity auction.

• Quiz night.

• Bring and buy sale.

• Church collection.

• Pack shoppers' bags at the supermarket.

• Dance 'till you drop' competition.

• Guess how many candies in the jar.

• Prize raffle.

• Orienteering challenge.

• Murder mystery meal.

• Wacky sports day.

I'm sure you can think of others.

Sponsored events

If you are organising a sponsored event, try to obtain sponsorship from local companies. Ask them to help practically, if it fits your theme. In my sponsored 'jailbreak' we had twenty-four hours in which to travel as far as possible from our starting point. A haulage company sponsored us £1 per mile covered, and we managed to hitch a 150-mile ride from a local car showroom. Any business links you have should be investigated to maximise your sponsorship. Ensure that their support is gratefully acknowledged with a thank-you letter after the event.

Sponsorship forms

The forms should have plenty of space for names and should look as official as possible. If you are a member of a club or society, for example a local athletics team, ask if you can use their official logo. Think about the design of the form. A scrawled table will not do – you don't want to be accused of trying to extract money with a sham scheme. I have included a sample sponsorship form in appendix II and also to download at www.degreesforfree.com..

Distribute the forms as widely as possible. Ask you parents to send them around their workplaces; give them to your friends, family and colleagues; get them into as many pubs, bars and clubs as you can.

Collecting the money

This can be a chore and it is highly likely that you will have to request money on several occasions before you get it. Leave yourself enough time to do this. Ensure everyone participating collects the money they were promised. People are notorious for forgetting to collect sponsorship monies once the excitement of the event has passed.

You might opt for a 'hit-and-run' approach by asking for money at the same time as people sign their names on the forms, but I leave this to your discretion. A local club might be obliging and keep a jar or collection tin on the bar for you.

Venue

Where are you going to hold your event? Unless you know someone who happens to have a gigantic spare room, you will need to book somewhere. And, again, you want to avoid spending your own money. Pubs may give you free hire of their function room for a mid-week event because they'll make money at the bar. Community centres and working men's clubs are another option. Try your local theatre for use of their auditorium on a free night, or host an event in the theatre bar. School halls and church halls are often available. For outdoor events, find a suitable car park, sports field, or pedestrianised area in your local shopping complex. Check that the hours in which you can use the venue are compatible with your plans, leaving plenty of time either side to set up and take down your equipment. Find out the maximum number of people that the venue can accommodate.

Check the venue's insurance policy – it may be worth spending £25, or $50 on insurance cover in case anything goes wrong and you are faced with a court case from an angry attendee. If you need a liquor licence, apply to the correct authorities well in advance to prevent disappointment. If your event will affect traffic, contact the local highways department. If it is taking place outside a theatre or other licensed performance venue and you are charging people, you might need a special licence. In the UK, for example, street theatre requires a licence from the local town council. Do fire hazards, exits and seating capacities require checking by the city authorities? Either way, the local council town or city hall will be able to help you. Will you be bothering any local residents with unnecessary noise? If your venue does not have an established policy or you are running your event late into the night, check restrictions with local authorities.

Volunteers

A large number of helpful, sensible friends are always a bonus when in need of voluntary help. In my experience, free entry and the offer of a drink usually guarantee support. If you are really stuck, call local volunteer networks and ask their advice. You will need to work out what you need. Do you need people on the door to take tickets? Do you need any bar staff? Do you need stewards or guides? If you anticipate a large turnout or your event is physical by nature, you could do with emergency first-aiders.

Make your volunteers noticeable to your audience by giving them similar clothing or official badges. Neon yellow vests are very cheap to buy these days and you may find a uniform supplier who is happy to let you borrow some. Also consider the needs of any children, elderly, or disabled attendees. Having one extra person on board to help specifically with these groups will help a large event to run more smoothly. Fully brief your helpers about what to do in an emergency – where fire exits and extinguishers are, where the first-aid kit lives. A pre-event briefing session is always a good idea and the information should also be given on handouts. If your event will span a large area, use walkie-talkies.

Performers and competitors

Like your helpers, your performers need to be fully briefed. Remember, if you keep them happy, they will help you in the future. What do they need? Obviously they will need to know the start and finish times and the running order. But do they require dressing rooms or practice space? How will they know when it's their turn to perform? If things are running behind schedule, who will tell them when to start? For physical events like charity fun-runs you will need refreshments and first-aid readily available.

Ill-informed performers will drop out, so keep in close contact with them leading up to the event. They will need handouts too, so they have the details in writing and can check them easily; and you save yourself having to answer the same question fifty times. If they do have any questions, answer them reassuringly – or if you don't know, tell them you'll find out from someone who does.

Publicity

To guarantee a good crowd, book things well in advance. This gives you plenty of time to publicise your event, send out press releases, sell advance tickets and phone everybody you've ever met to get them to come. Don't spend money on lavish flyers – photocopy them or get a printing company to print them for free. Word of mouth, personal recommendations and reputations are the real key to pulling in a crowd.

If you are afraid of the telephone, get over it, or get someone else to ring round for you!

Technical requirements

It is surprising how the obvious can be overlooked, for instance electricity, water, lighting… Will you need any of them? Are they available at your venue? Will you need someone to set up and operate electrical equipment.

If you need equipment, such as a personal address system, loudspeaker, sound amplifier, etc, and neither you nor the venue has such things, try and see if a local company will lend them to you. In fact scrounging is often the best way to get your equipment together and it is for a good cause – you.

Hospitality

You would be surprised how many people reach into their pockets at the mention of a free buffet included in the price. Again, you don't need exquisite catering. If you, your friends and family all bring a few plates of stuff, there will be plenty to go around. Other attractions are free drinks, a late bar, or the chance to win something.

Pay-as-you-play and other money making spin-offs

A raffle can add a couple of hundred pounds or dollars to your takings. Of course a raffle requires prizes – see 'donated goods and raffle prizes'. Other ideas for pay-as-you-play spin-offs are scratch cards, competitions, quizzes, auctions, programmes, or souvenirs for sale. I recommend asking for goods to be donated for raffle prizes and competitions rather than buying them yourself.

The horrible bit

Tidying up. You have to do it, so ask your volunteers to stay behind afterwards to help you, unless you want to be stranded alone in a field with four huge speakers to lift by yourself. Make sure there is transport to return all the equipment and, if it's a late finish, that your helpers have some way of getting home!

Future improvements

With good preparation, your event will run smoothly. There are always improvements and new ideas to be made so a post-event debriefing or evaluation will provide feedback from your volunteers, participants and performers. They will want to know how successful you were in raising money. You might choose to distribute evaluation forms – sometimes people find it hard to speak up in a meeting.

Post-event report

People appreciate being told how their support has helped, so inform all participants of your success afterwards. Tell everybody exactly how much you made in total. Put something up on a notice board if you want to thank a number of people who work or meet in the same place. Thank any business that has sponsored or helped you – this is common courtesy and could guarantee their support in the future.

With detailed preparation, your event will succeed. Problems may occur on the day itself, but you can tackle them as they arrive. That's half the fun of live events – they are a very rewarding and proactive way to raise money and it's really heart warming to see friends, family and complete strangers rally to support your cause.

Checklist

✔ Have you set a financial target and chosen a theme?

✔ Have you chosen a date that gives you time to organise the event properly and that doesn't clash with something else?

✔ Have you contacted local businesses for sponsorship?

✔ Have you organised a venue?

✔ Have you checked any legal requirements: insurance, maximum attendance, licensing, fire safety, noise restrictions?

✔ Do you have enough volunteers to staff your event?

✔ Have you briefed your volunteers properly and organised official badges for them to wear?

✔ Have you organised refreshments?

✔ Have you spread the word and made flyers or tickets?

✔ Do you know your technical requirements?

✔ Have your sorted out prizes for raffles and spin-offs?

✔ Have you organised volunteers for the tidying up and made sure that everyone can get home afterwards?

✔ Have you sorted out a date for a post-event briefing?

Chapter nine

Goods, donations and raffle prizes

You are going to need a good many things for your education. Identify any material items that can be bought – food, travel passes, books, sporting equipment and the tools of your trade. Cost each item. If a company or individual could donate that piece of equipment, you would save pounds. Think in equivalent terms, for example, 'If I had a bicycle, I could save £500 per annum on travel fares.'

Using the telephone directory, highlight twenty or so appropriate businesses for each item. Local shopkeepers are just as likely to help as national chain stores. Make a telephone call to find out the name of the person you need to contact, checking the address and contact details. You only need to find out information, you will not be requesting anything over the phone. Although not essential, it helps to have the name of a society or club to mention because it sounds official. And make sure you have a script in front of you. For example:

> 'I'm calling from the Gary Amateur Dramatics Society about fundraising. We'd like to write to you with more information, so could I take the name of the manager? And may I check your address?'

If the person you are speaking to wants more information, or you find yourself speaking to the manager, explain that a member of your group has been offered a study opportunity and needs use of fencing equipment, a bicycle, or whatever, and that you will send full details in the post. It is important to stress that you are sending something in writing. This will put the manager's mind at rest because a) a letter on headed paper is official and b) pushy telephone sales people are the bane of everyone's life.

You then need to compose a letter in the same way as you would approach a business or charitable foundation – explaining your background, present situation and need, how their donation will help and what they will receive in return. None of the equipment needs to be brand new, provided it is in full working order, so you should make this clear. If you can, use the logo of any club, society, or school you belong to. Don't go overboard; donors are not the same as sponsors and will not expect any great favours in return. If you are suddenly asked, 'What's in it for me?' by a donor, suggest a press release and photo opportunity in the local paper. Then contact your journalist friend, who by now should know your first name and favourite colour!

Make a follow-up telephone call two or three days afterwards. Speak to the manager, check that the details arrived and ask if the company would be able to help. Repeat that a fully working, second-hand item would be perfect.

With any luck, you will save yourself some money.

Raffle prizes

Raffles are an ideal way to boost the takings of an event. You do not need loads of goods; three decent prizes are enough to persuade someone to part with twenty pence. Try and link your prizes to the theme of your event if possible; for example, a Shakespeare Night's prizes could include a pair of tickets to your local theatre, a copy of Shakespeare's Collected Sonnets, a free meal at the local bar 'The Shakespeare' and a crate of traditional English beer.

Make a list of prizes and a list of companies who may be able to supply them. Take advantage of any contacts you have – if an uncle runs a shop, ask him if he could donate a few bottles of something.

One advantage for companies is that you will mention their name each time you announce the prizes – a good bit of cheap publicity. You should also offer complimentary tickets for your event to each company. This makes it seem like they are getting something out of it and is a fun way to get them involved. Who knows? They might help again next year.

Make telephone enquiries first to establish whom you should talk to. Explain your situation and your event to them and ask if they could help. If you are asked to submit something in writing, take down the relevant details. If you have a shopping centre nearby, it may save time to go in and speak to the manager of each shop. If you decide to 'cold call', take a formal letter that confirms that the goods donated will be used as raffle prizes for a fundraising event. A letter from the venue, a club you belong to, or your prospective school or college would be ideal.

After the event, it is common courtesy to contact each company and thank them for their support. They will then be more inclined to help you again.

Checklist

✔ **Have you listed and costed all items you need for your course?**

✔ **Can you identify twenty businesses that might help?**

✔ **Have you written a script for your initial phone calls?**

✔ **Have you drafted a request letter on headed paper?**

✔ **Have you made a list and script for follow-up phone calls?**

Chapter ten

Writing to individuals

Although you want to raise money, you also want to raise awareness of the plight of students up and down the country. If enough political support were gained to guarantee funding for all students, there would be no need for this guide. You can lobby the government nationally and your local government representative may offer useful advice about raising the profile of your campaign. These days it is easy to start a petition on the internet and use social networking sites to highlight your plea.

Non-financial support

There are other influential individuals who may be able to help you. The late Charlton Heston agreed to give a free interview to a drama student who was in financial difficulty. That student was then able to make money by selling the interview.

While I am not suggesting you write to hundreds of celebrities, there are ways in which sympathisers of some standing can contribute to your cause without donating money. Ask a local news presenter to give a talk at your fundraising debate evening, or a local football club player could open your fun-run – it's up to you.

Financial support

Financial support from individuals is referred to as 'patronage'. Patronage is purely for the good of the community and a patron forgoes the benefits that a sponsor would receive.

It will be of benefit to write to any wealthy individual in your family or circle of friends. Apart from that, your research should revolve around the types of individuals you wish to write to. Landowners, chief executives, musicians, peers, entrepreneurs, film directors, lottery winners... the list is endless. You will, once again, need to visit your local library with a jumbo-sized jotter and a couple of hours set aside. Build a profile of your ideal patron, e.g. 'born in the West Midlands region, earns over £5m, supports arts and music'.

Although some students have received support from celebrities or renowned scholars, any well-known individual will receive hundreds of funding requests from students each year. If someone is dedicated to supporting the plight of students, it is likely that he or she will make a contribution direct to a school or university. Contact your school to see if they approve of you contacting established graduates. Of course, if you have a personal link with someone well known that's a different matter.

Once you have built a profile of your patron and checked the contact details, you should submit a letter similar to that for donations from charitable foundations. Don't write again or telephone them – if they want to help they will contact you.

Checklist

✔ **Have you contacted local and national government representatives?**

✔ **Have you started an online petition?**

✔ **Can you list local celebrities connected to your cause?**

✔ **Have you made a list of wealthy individuals you know personally?**

✔ **Have you used the local library or internet to identify potential patrons?**

Chapter eleven

Communicating effectively and saying thank you

By now you will already have developed new skills in communicating. Clarity is essential when dealing with business proposals, organising events, applications to charitable foundations and trusts – and although there are no set rules, here are some guidelines for obtaining information and expressing your needs.

Telephone enquiries

Telephones are for information, not decisions. Companies in particular resent feeling compelled to make financial decisions over the telephone – if you've ever received a call from a salesman you will understand. Telephone enquiries are the best way to refine your searches and target sources of income. Rather than sending out twenty sponsorship letters to businesses to 'test the water', make a telephone call to the appropriate person in each and ask about the company's policy on charitable giving. Perhaps five companies will prove worth an application and now you will be able to approach them on an individual basis. You will know how you fare within their guidelines, as well as reducing your printing, photocopying and postage costs.

Don't fluff your words. Before you make the call, know what you want to find out. Have information to hand in case your contact has any queries. A script and some brief notes are useful.

For example:

To the receptionist: 'Could you put me through to the person dealing with charitable enquiries, please?'

To the right person: 'Are you the person responsible for making charitable donations? Please may I have a copy of your guidelines, or an application form?'

Confirm names and addresses, spellings and deadlines.

My information in brief: Individual studying at Universal College. Three-year diploma, starts September 20. Living in Leicester. Parents a builder and a nurse. No government grants available, turned down for funding. Raising fees through combination of donations, sponsorship and events. Raised £10,000 so far. Looking for £500 for travel expenses. Any help gratefully received. Will write.

Have paper and a pen ready to write down the information. Try to avoid long pauses and phrases like 'erm', 'basically' and 'I'm not sure'. Always sound positive, friendly and confident that you know what you're talking about. This puts people at ease. If the other person sounds unsure, explain your cause briefly and ask if they would like further written information in the post. Never give misleading or false information because you think it will benefit your cause – it will conflict with your written information and you don't want to come across as a con artist.

To clarify further action, reiterate any requests before you put the telephone down. For example:

'Just to confirm... you want me to get hold of the arts editor and find a suitable angle and deadline for the story. In the meantime you'll speak to Nidal and decide what kind of support you can offer us, am I right?

I'll get back to you with those details and a time to meet, is that okay?'

As you can see, this helps to prevent misunderstandings and crossed wires.

Letters and written information

There is a standard format for business letters. An example is available in appendix II and also to download free at www.degreesforfree.com. Dig out any official letters you or your family have received and you will see the similarities in layout and style. Presentation of your information is as important as content. Use a serif typeface, as they are much easier to read. Serif means there are semi-structural differences (curly bits!). This book is mainly in a serif face, statements 1 and 2 below use sans serif. It's best not to use too many gimmicks, such as too much underlining, subheadings, or too many exclamation points. You want your letter to look as personal as possible, rather than a mass mailing. Avoid the passive tense and express yourself briefly and definitely. Look at the difference in these two statements:

Statement 1:

'If you want, it might be good to meet, perhaps at a time convenient to you, to talk about what you think. Let me know if you agree.'

Statement 2:

'I would like to arrange a meeting to discuss the proposal. When would be best?'

The second is the most dynamic. Adopt a more friendly tone if you know your contact personally.

Many businesses now close their letters with 'Best wishes' or 'With regards', but traditionally use 'Yours sincerely' for named contacts and 'Yours faithfully' if you are writing to Sir/Madam (which, of course, you shouldn't be doing).

If you are finding it hard to phrase something, set out the minimum information and then try and fill in the gaps. Writing succinctly is a skill and requires practice. You will have plenty of that!

Provided your covering letter is personal, save yourself time by photocopying your budget, strategy document and supporting information. I put together an A5 pamphlet detailing my background and situation, which saved me a great deal of time when writing to businesses. A sample leaflet is available to download for free at www.degreesforfree.com

Keep copies of your master documents for your fundraising campaigns in future years.

A very important letter

I have mentioned saying thank you several times throughout this book, but I cannot stress how important this is to all fundraisers, whether they are professionals, or not.

When we're children we are taught to say thank you properly. No one liked doing it, but it was a necessity if we wanted to be sure to get another present. Some times we genuinely wanted to show our appreciation.

When raising money, a sure way to get a second donation is to say thank you properly. The letters should be personal and should be sent within a few days of receiving the donation. You should confirm that the money will be used as the donor intended and, if it wasn't specified you should say how you will use it. If someone has sponsored an event, or donated goods, you can write afterwards to tell them how it went. Never use a thank-you letter to ask for more money.

It might be an idea to say thank you formally to your volunteers as well.

There are lots of creative ways to thank people. I sent a newsletter every term to every donor – whether corporate, charitable foundation, or someone that I knew – updating them on my progress and thanking them again for their contribution. In the final year, I also invited each donor to my college open days, offering them free tickets to my theatrical performances. I also gave the names and details to the college bursar, who sent them a glossy college brochure every year with an official thank-you letter from the school.

It's important to remember who has helped you, not just for fundraising purposes, but for life in general. As a working adult I make a habit of donating whenever I can. As my income has increased, I have begun to tithe – give away – ten percent of my salary to charity. Recently I ran a half-marathon and raised £1,377 for SOS Children. One year I asked my family and friends to donate all of my Christmas presents to charity because I felt life had been pretty good to me and that actually I didn't need anything. And in the grand scheme of things, these are very small contributions to make.

Right now you are asking people to help you. Somewhere, there are other people in the world who you can help. While right now your priority is in funding your own education, at some point in the future you will be in a position to help somebody else.

Being grateful, saying thank you and giving something back are all extremely positive things to do. You can't help but feel good when you say thank you, or give an unexpected gift. These simple acts will not only make your donors feel good, but will make you feel good and bring positivity into your own life.

Checklist

✔ **Do you have a script for all your telephone enquiries?**

✔ **Did you repeat all requirements at the end of each phone call as confirmation and to avoid confusion?**

✔ **Do you use an appropriate formal style for covering letters?**

✔ **Have you kept copies of all your master documents?**

✔ **Does your thank-you letter sound genuine?**

✔ **Have you thanked your volunteers?**

Chapter twelve

The last straw

Why saddle yourself with debt when you can raise the money? As a last resort, you could always get a loan, but, hopefully, you will not need it.

Local authorities in the UK sometimes pay towards the living or housing costs of certain students, including lone parents, students with dependant children, disabled students and part-time students. Partners of students may also apply. Contact your local authority for more information.

Some foundations and trusts offer loans as an option to grants. It might also be worth talking to your bank manager about the services the bank can offer you.

Like me, you can manage to raise the money to pay for your education. It is hard work and at times dispiriting; on the other hand it is challenging, often tremendous fun – and great for your social life. I cannot explain how rewarding it feels to see people come together to raise the money needed for your training. Your organisational skills will be practised and fearsome. You will be prepared for marketing your abilities after graduation.

Organise and keep copies of everything – all of your master documents, all of the addresses and phone numbers of your contacts and all of their replies, whether favourable or not. Once you plunge into your studies, it may be easy to forget your responsibilities to your sponsors. Their details need to be readily available for those termly reports. You may have to return to fundraising during each summer holiday and you will need the contact details you gathered before.

Good luck and all the best with your career. *You can do it!*

Appendix I

Student information

United Kingdom
www.degreesforfree.com.
www.nusonline.co.uk
www.gotouni.direct.gov.uk
www.dius.gov.uk
www.family-action.org.uk
www.egas.online.org
www.funderfinder.org.uk
www.volresource.org.uk

South Africa
www.studysa.co.za
www.southafrica.info/about/education

United States
www.students.gov

Canada
www.campusaccess.com
www.cicic.ca

Australia
www.studentservices.com.au
www.goingtouni.gov.au
www.australianscholarships.gov.au

New Zealand
www.students.org.nz
www.studenthub.co.nz

Charity and sponsorship books

United Kingdom
Guide to the Major Trusts - Vol I and II
Educational Grants Directory
Directory of Grant-Making Trusts
The Funders' Almanac

Directory of Social Change
24 Stephenson Way
London NW1 2DP

www.dsc.org.uk

Hollis Sponsorship and Donations Year Book
Hollis UK Public Relations Annual

WBI Media & Entertainment
Paulton House
8 Shepherdess Walk
London N1 7LB

www.hollis-publishing.com

Charity Choice
The Charities Digest

Waterlow Professional Publishing
Paulton House
8 Shepherdess Walk
London N1 7LB

www.charitychoice.co.uk

Hobsons Sponsorship Yearbook

Hobsons Publishing PLC
Bateman Street

Cambrdge CB2 1LZ
Tel: 01223 354551

United States and Canada
Annual Register of Grant Support

Information Today Inc.
143 Old Marlton Pike
Medford, NJ 08055-8750
Tel: 609-654-6266

www.infotoday.com/directories

Worldwide

Tiny Essentials of Fundraising
Tiny Essentials of Writing for Fundraising
Tiny Essentials of Major Gift Fundraising
Tiny Essentials of Raising Money from Foundations and Trusts
Tiny Essentials of a Fundraising Strategy

The White Lion Press Ltd
567 Ben Jonson House
The Barbican
London EC2Y 8NH
www.whitelionpress.com

Grants Register

Palgrave Macmillan UK and Europe
Houndmills
Basingstoke
Hampshire RG21 6XS
Tel: 01256 329242

www.palgrave.com

Palgrave Macmillan US
175 Fifth Avenue
New York
NY 10010
Tel: 1 (888) 330-8477
www.palgrave-usa.com

Palgrave Macmillan Australia
Postal Locked Bag 1,
Prahran
Victoria
Australia 3181
Tel: 61 3 9825 1111
www.palgravemacmillan.com.au

Palgrave Macmillan South Africa
P.O. Box 31487
Braamfontein
Johannesburg
2017 South Africa
Tel: 11 731 3300
www.palgrave.com

Appendix II

All the examples here are also available to download free of charge, in either Word or pdf format, at www.degreesforfree.com, which is full of information on how to fund your degree. You can also join the discussions about student finances and raising funds for your own training.

Sample press release

FOR IMMEDIATE RELEASE

Fundraising LAD girl back in Shakespeare's country!

STRATFORD, Warwickshire. – June 2008 – After her first year of training at the London Academy of Drama, local girl Bryony Weir has returned to Stratford to work with the Stratford Youth Theatre on their new Shakespeare project.

'It's good to be home for the holidays and to be working with the Youth Theatre again. My six years as a member were the reason I got into LAD, now I want to share my experiences with them. It's been an amazing first year, I'm stunned by how much I've learned and how much I still have to learn.'

The principal of LAD, Barry Nicholas, said: 'Bryony is an excellent student and is highly regarded by both students and staff. She is making excellent progress in all aspects of the course and has wonderful potential.'

Faced with disaster twelve months ago when she couldn't afford the £40,000 it costs to train at drama school, Bryony rose to the challenge and has raised a staggering £23,000 to date from a combination of fundraising events, sponsorship and donations.

'Really it was through necessity – I knew I had to find the money or turn down my place. It's been hard, but my friends, family and local people have been incredible and I couldn't have done it without their support. I'm so glad I had to fundraise – it has taught me a great deal about dealing with the media and promoting myself – all skills I'll need as an actor.'

LAD is one of the top drama schools in the country and over 1,500 people audition for one of thirty precious places. Past students include Fred Fiennes, Jerry Hopkins and Amelia Redgrave.

'We are being trained for theatre, radio, TV and film to the highest standards, so I think I'll be spoilt for choice when I leave. London is a very exciting place but I love Stratford and one of my ambitions is to work here after LAD.'

But it's a race against the clock – Bryony must raise another £4,000 before September 21st if she is to continue into her second year:

'I know I'll do it. When I finish my training I know I will go on to do great things. That's why I'm seeking sponsorship from a local company who would benefit from being linked to LAD and the next generation of exciting young acting talent.'

The Youth Theatre's Shakespeare project 'Arrant Knaves and Bawdy Wenches' will be performed in Hamlet's Restaurant at the Stratford Theatre on 13th September. Tickets are £5 and £3 and are available from the box office on Stratford 566055.

Interview contact: Bryony Weir on Stratford 890211.

Bryony Weir
7 Lakeside Row
Stratford
CV32 5HH

Sample sponsorship form

PRESTON GIRLS' SCHOOL

22 OLDCROFT ROAD, PRESTON P11 2DJ

SPONSORED JAILBREAK

20th AUGUST 2008

To raise much-needed funds to send Maureen Grant to the Royal Veterinary School. Please help by making a donation, large or small. All monies must be collected by September 16th 2008.

Name	Address	Amount per mile	Max amount

Sample sponsorship letter

Your name
Your address
Your telephone number

Jim Shanks
Secretary to the Board
GefCo PLC
Mockers House
PO Box 10
Bridgemouth
BR72 5RF

4 August 2008

Dear Mr Shanks

My name is Rita Smith. I have enclosed a leaflet giving you a little more information on my background and situation.

I strive for excellence in engineering and am seeking a partnership with GefCo for their similar beliefs. This is an exciting sponsorship opportunity linking the prestige of the Brunel College of Engineers, the next generation of young engineering talent and the most forward-thinking vehicle manufacturer in the UK.

There are two options for sponsorship that I ask you to consider:

• **Option 1 – GefCo as major sponsor**

GefCo agree to partner my training at BCE, becoming my official and sole sponsor. The cost is £3,500 per year and the sponsorship will last for two years.

• Option 2 – GefCo as donor of travel expenses

GefCo agree to donate £100 to subsidise my travel expenses.

In becoming my official sponsor, GefCo would benefit from full acknowledgement in all BCE publications, including the BCE prospectus, BCE Magazine and programmes for all productions. These publications are distributed to every engineering professional and company in the UK.

This option includes a major media announcement to all local press, radio and TV stations and repeat exposure for the duration of the sponsorship. For the two years following my graduation, my curriculum vitae will formally acknowledge GefCo as my sponsor, and will be circulated to all major engineering companies.

Together with this increased profile, representatives from GefCo will be invited to attend all BCE events and open days. GefCo will also receive a specially designed sponsor pack, including a certificate and photographs for your use together with a termly report on my progress.

The second option involves GefCo agreeing to cover my travel expenses. In return for your generous donation you will receive a certificate and report on my progress throughout the coming year.

The benefits to myself will be, of course, enormous – I will be able to continue my training and launch into a dynamic career, not only at a national level, but locally.

One of my ambitions is to return to Bridgemouth to work with local young people and schools on educational and fun engineering projects, giving this important part of our modern life new relevance within society.

Over the last twelve months I have successfully raised over £27,000 to fund my training at the most prestigious school of its kind. I would like GefCo to share in this achievement, and I hope that together we can play a part in shaping the future of performance in the UK.

My proposal is that we should meet to discuss the potential for sponsorship. I can be contacted at the address above or during working hours on (01244) 590078.

Thank you for your consideration.

Best wishes
Rita Smith

Doreen Hughes

Selected from over 1,400 candidates for the Royal College of Science and Technology

Like most children, I loved building things. For hours I would make towers from wooden blocks or bend leftover bits of plastic into crazy vehicles. I let my imagination run riot. Then I realised I could actually design smaller versions of buildings or machines that people could actually use. Over the years this grew into an incredible love of engineering...

Doreen Hughes

In 2004 I won the Bristol City Award for Innovative Technical Design. In the same year, my team was the winner of the Creative Sparks competition with our hovercraft design. I spent the following year as an apprentice with Rolls Royce. I was thrilled when I was accepted at the Royal College of Science and Technology because it meant I could realise my ambitions.

'Doreen is an instinctive young engineer with a talent that must be developed.'

Iain Salisbury, Rolls Royce Head of Engineering

The Royal College of Science and Technology

The Royal College of Science and Technology originated as the Glasgow and West of Scotland Technical College, which was formed in 1887 from the amalgamation of Anderson's College, the College of Science and Arts, Allan Glen's Institution, the Young Chair of Technical Chemistry and Atkinson's Institution. After seeking permission from King George V in 1912, the College changed its name to the Royal Technical College. In 1956 there was another change of name for the College and it became the Royal College of Science and Technology. Under the recommendation of the Robbins Committee, the Scottish College of Commerce amalgamated with the College to form the University of Strathclyde in 1964.

Over the years, the RCST has produced some of the world's finest engineering talent, like Richard

Doreen Hughes

Cauldwell, Ned Hoover and Tetsuo Nissan. As such, young engineers from all over the world try to gain places at the RCST

Funding

Bristol Local Education Authority does not recognise this course as eligible for a discretionary grant. RCST is a registered charity (no. 66125) and can offer only very limited financial assistance. My family cannot afford to pay the fees and I have to raise the tuition fees and maintenance costs myself. Determined not to let this stop me, I have launched a fundraising campaign and I hope to raise the £16,000 I need to cover my costs for the first year.

TUITION FEES per year	£8,595
ACCOMMODATION per year	£4,680
MAINTENANCE per year	£2,856
TOTAL: £16,131	

I have already raised £2,768 towards this figure. If I do not cover the shortfall, I will not be able to attend RCST.

Fundraising

I have established a trust fund and I am trying to attract local and business sponsorship. I have applied to charitable foundations and trusts, contacted individuals for patronage and I am organising schools' workshops, car boot sales and entertainment nights to raise the money. I have also managed to save £1,000 from my own earnings.

Doreen Hughes

How You Can Help

✔ By becoming a patron.

✔ By donating goods for car boot sales.

✔ By sponsoring my training.

✔ By making a donation.

An account has been set up in the name of the
Miss D Hughes Training Fund for this purpose.

In return for your sponsorship, you will be invited to
all RCST events, credited in all of their publications
and all of my campaign publicity, receive a specially
designed certificate and an annual report on my
progress at RCST. Any donation, however small or
great, will be gratefully received.

I am indebted to the following for their kind support
and encouragement: Janice Bassett, the Rooney
Trust, Keith McIntyre, Lila Myers, INJ Blurings,
Rolls Royce and all at Bristol College.

If you can offer any help or advice, please get in
touch.

If you can't help right now, thank you for reading. I
would be grateful if you could pass this on to a friend
with an interest in engineering.

Yours sincerely,

Doreen Hughes

23 Jotherswalk Road
Bristol
B11 4TT

Sample business letter

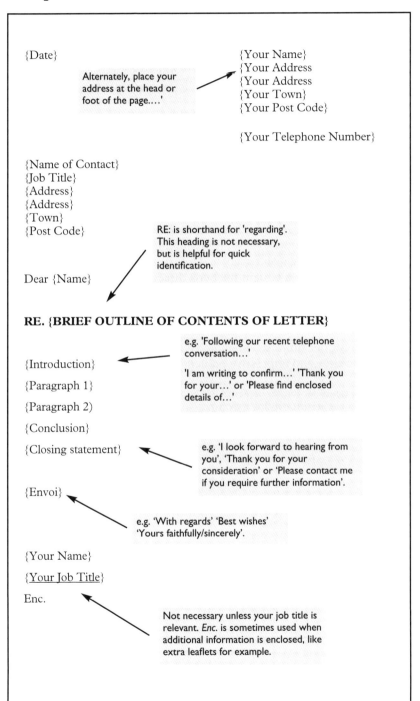

{Date}

Alternately, place your address at the head or foot of the page....'

{Your Name}
{Your Address
{Your Address
{Your Town}
{Your Post Code}

{Your Telephone Number}

{Name of Contact}
{Job Title}
{Address}
{Address}
{Town}
{Post Code}

RE: is shorthand for 'regarding'. This heading is not necessary, but is helpful for quick identification.

Dear {Name}

RE. {BRIEF OUTLINE OF CONTENTS OF LETTER}

e.g. 'Following our recent telephone conversation...'

{Introduction}

'I am writing to confirm...' 'Thank you for your...' or 'Please find enclosed details of...'

{Paragraph 1}

{Paragraph 2)

{Conclusion}

{Closing statement}

e.g. 'I look forward to hearing from you', 'Thank you for your consideration' or 'Please contact me if you require further information'.

{Envoi}

e.g. 'With regards' 'Best wishes' 'Yours faithfully/sincerely'.

{Your Name}

{Your Job Title}

Enc.

Not necessary unless your job title is relevant. *Enc.* is sometimes used when additional information is enclosed, like extra leaflets for example.

A promise from
The White Lion Press

Enjoy the best books on fundraising and voluntary sector development.

Books by The White Lion Press will repay your investment many times over – and you'll enjoy reading them too. But if your purchase is damaged in any way, or if you feel any of our products do not live up to your expectations simply return them to us and we will issue you with a full refund, including any reasonable associated costs. We'll ask you to tell us why, so we can put right anything that might be wrong, but we won't quibble. Unfortunately we can only offer this if you bought the book directly from us, but even if you didn't, please let us know your problem and we'll do all we can to ensure your supplier matches our commitment to you. After all, you are our ultimate customer.

We further promise to handle your orders with speed, efficiency and impressive politeness.

You can order further copies of this book, or any of our other titles, from our secure website, www.whitelionpress.com. If you prefer, you can order by email, orders@whitelionpress.com.

Tiny Essentials of Fundraising

by Neil Sloggie
Softback, 57 pp. ISBN 0-9518971-5-2

All you really need to know about
fundraising, in one tiny book.

Join Kate, an inquisitive and ambitious
new recruit to the fundraising
profession, as she sets out to uncover
what really matters in her chosen career
by visiting and asking three seasoned practitioners. Like
Kate you'll see as much to avoid as to emulate in the first
two encounters but you'll be reassured and inspired as, in
her final meeting, Kate discovers an organisation that has
really thought through its fundraising strategy and
approach, and shares with her – and you – the essential
secrets of fundraising success.

'A simple and truthful reminder of what's at the heart of effective fundraising.
How I wish someone had given me this book when I was starting out all those
years ago!'
Jan Chisholm, managing director, Pareto Fundraising, Australia.

'I was given a copy of the "Tiny" book in Australia and was so enamoured of the
clear message it conveys that I ordered a special edition to give to more than
1,500 fundraisers and all 700 Blackbaud employees. Their reactions have been
universally positive. *Tiny Essentials of Fundraising* is one of those books that make
us truly envious of the author for executing such a brilliant piece of writing...'
Robert Sywolski, former chief executive, Blackbaud Inc, USA.

'It's a smart idea, well-executed – how fabulous to have a bite-sized book that
sums up what makes for successful fundraising in such an accessible way to both
native and non-native English speakers.'

'Great stuff. Thanks Neil for what must be the shortest, simplest and yet very
salient contribution to the world's literature on fundraising.'
Julie Weston, UNHCR, Switzerland.

Tiny Essentials of Writing for Fundraising

by George Smith

Softback, 65 pp.
ISBN 0-9518971-6-0

'I suggest your heart would soar if – once in a while – you received a letter written in decent English which said unexpected things in elegant ways, which moved you and stirred your emotions, which angered you or made you proud, a letter apparently written by one individual to another individual. For you never see these letters any more…'

If you believe that words matter then this opinionated little book is for you. For this 'Tiny' book will change forever the way you and your organisation communicate.

'*Tiny Essentials of Writing for Fundraising* is a refreshing – and delightfully short – guide to the author's insights about the writer's craft. If you're even thinking about writing fundraising letters you can't afford not to buy this remarkable little book.'
Mal Warwick, chairman, Mal Warwick & Associates Inc, USA.

'I am a huge fan of George's blunt but refined writing, his clear and individual voice, and his extraordinary ability to cut through the crap – keep this wonderful little book next to your pen and pc.'
Lyndall Stein, CEO, Concern, UK.

'Smith is a self-confessed curmudgeon but nobody describes better than he the power of words to advance your cause. The 11,149 words in this lovely book have been carefully selected and assembled to help you write well enough to convince anyone of anything.'
Ken Burnett, author, *the Zen of Fundraising*.

Tiny Essentials of Major Gift Fundraising

by Neil Sloggie
Softback, 61 pp. ISBN 0-9518971-7-9

The natural successor to his first book, *Tiny Essentials of Fundraising*, this time Neil Sloggie tells the story of Daniel, who had never thought of asking any donor individually for money, nor of asking for more than a three-figure sum. Join him in his search to uncover the Holy Grail of major gift fundraising and learn as he did how to secure donations bigger than a house – and lots of them.

This 'Tiny' contains in their purest, most distilled form the priceless secrets of a neglected area of vast fundraising potential.

'Help is close at hand in this small gem – wise counsel, the importance of colleagues and networking, heaps of practical advice. To borrow Neil's words, "keep this one near the top of your priority pile".'
Sue-Anne Wallace, chief executive officer, Fundraising Institute-Australia.

'… a really helpful guide, especially to someone just starting out or wishing to do a quick reappraisal of their operation.'
Nick Booth, campaign director, NSPCC 'Full Stop' campaign, UK.

Tiny Essentials of an Effective Volunteer Board

by Ken Burnett
Softback, 81 pp. ISBN 0-9518971-8-7

When Warren Maxwell is suddenly propelled into the chairman's seat of the voluntary organisation on whose board he serves, he decides that his somewhat mediocre board is going to become a paragon of all that's excellent in nonprofit governance. Join him on his brief, eventful, enlightening quest to discover what makes a balanced, progressive and highly effective volunteer board.

'This excellent and very readable book is essential for every board member of a charity. I realise how much better a chair and trustee I could have been if only the book had been written 30 years earlier.'
Lord Joel Joffe, former chair of trustees, Oxfam UK.

'This tiny book is a huge contribution to the literature on governing boards. Told as a compelling story, the insights and experience-based facts are woven skilfully throughout. A delight to read, the lessons fly off the page.'
Kay Sprinkel Grace, author, *Beyond Fundraising* and *The Ultimate Board Member's Book*, USA.

'This energising, readable book draws out what's really important, the true "tiny essentials". The 21 keys summarised in chapter six are the cream on the cake...'
Noerine Kaleeba, chair of trustees, ActionAid International, South Africa.

'This little book is absolutely brilliant; it's easy to read and is full of useful information on how to improve the effectiveness of trustee boards.'

'I found this book to be a very informative resource. I loved the style; to have a fictional story to read certainly drove home the salient points far more than a dull, factual text could have done and I found this approach to be very warm and engaging.'
Tracy Saunders, information officer, in *Volunteering Magazine* July 2006, UK.

'In every field there are those who become the "philosophers" of their fields. Burnett is such a philosopher for the field of fundraising. He is, in essence, a "guru".'

'Burnett's new book is appropriate for his status as fundraising guru since it exhibits the wisdom and in-depth thinking that is characteristic of one who is steeped in the history, philosophy, and literature of the field.'
Joanne Fritz, in a review on the website Nonprofit Charitable Orgs (part of the New York Times Group) August 2006, USA.

Tiny Essentials of Monthly Committed Giving

by Harvey McKinnon
Softback, 70 pp. ISBN-13: 978-0-9553993 0-5;
ISBN-10: 0-9553993-0-0

This book clearly describes the secrets of committed giving, what they are and what they require. In an entertaining, readable yet practical way, the author shares his insights, experience and wisdom. You can start by benefiting from this simple yet superbly effective fundraising proposition in not much longer than the 60 minutes or so it will take you to read this book.

'I read this Tiny book on the bus and made heads turn by laughing out loud several times. It is easy to read, easy to understand and will be easy to use since the 43 best ideas are summed up at the end. Veteran fundraiser Harvey McKinnon even gives you the answers to convince your mule of a boss that it is time to try monthly giving, now.'
Joan Flanagan, author, *Successful Fundraising*, USA.

'Everyone has time to read a tiny book and after you read this one, you'll be able to raise lots more money for your cause through setting up a monthly donor program. This is one of the best uses of an hour that I can think of.'
Rosemary Oliver, development director, Amnesty International, Canada.

'Harvey McKinnon's latest book is a kind of bedtime story for sleepless adults – those who run financially-strapped nonprofits. If you read it tonight, you'll sleep more peacefully. Tomorrow, you'll start raising more money.'
Andy Robinson, author, *Big Gifts for Small Groups and Grassroots Grants*, USA.

'This tiny guide has given philanthropy a huge gift. McKinnon's entertaining style whilst sharing his formidable fundraising skills is in itself an act of selfless generosity.'
Lelei LeLaulu, president, Counterpart International; chairman, Foundation of the Peoples of the South Pacific, Canada.

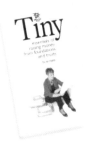

Tiny Essentials of Raising Money from Foundations and Trusts

by Jo Habib
Softback, 77 pp.
ISBN 0-9518971-9-5

Of all the world's major donors (and they are major, giving away £33 billion plus each year in the UK and USA alone), foundations and trusts may be the most pure. They have no function other than to give their money away. In *Tiny Essentials of Raising Money from Foundations and Trusts*, Jo Habib shows you with precision how to get your share.

'This book brings clarity to a world that is often apparently obscure and will help anyone understand the steps that need to be taken when approaching others for money. Written clearly and simply it will be invaluable both to the novice and to experienced old hands who think they really understand their target market. It is definitely essential reading.'
Julia Unwin, consultant and author, *The Grant-Making Tango*, UK.

'This is an encyclopaedia on fundraising from foundations and trusts packed into a tiny book. Jo Habib covers everything a new fundraiser will need to know, with admirable clarity, thoroughness and authority. Experienced fundraisers should also refer to this splendid guide, using it as a check list against which to review their own practice.'
David Carrington, consultant, UK.

Tiny Essentials of a Fundraising Strategy

(to be published summer 2009)

by Maggie Taylor and Ilene Hoyle
Softback, approx 65 pp.
ISBN-13: 978-0-9553993-2-9;
ISBN-10: 0-9553993-2-7

Strategy scares people, because it sounds like it should involve something substantial, like a war or at least an invasion. But at its heart strategy is just knowing where you want to get to and working out the best way to get there.

In this Tiny book Maggie Taylor and Ilene Hoyle have stripped away all the mystique and mystery, replacing it with a logical, straightforward and fun account of why a sound strategy matters, how you can go about getting one and how you can make sure it works for you and your organisation.

'A small book full of big fundraising questions – with answers on every page. A must read for those responsible for fundraising strategy in small and large organisations.'
Jo Swinhoe, director of fundraising and marketing, Alzheimer's Society, UK.

'This takes the fear out of the challenges of fundraising planning and strategy with a worked example fundraisers everywhere can relate to. Another tiny guide that punches above its weight.'
Adrian Sargeant, Robert F Hartsook Professor of Fundraising,
Indiana University-Purdue University, USA.

'Short, simple and effective. A pain free way to think about developing and implementing your fundraising strategy.'
Jonathon Grapsas, regional director, Pareto Fundraising, Canada.

The Zen of Fundraising

by Ken Burnett
Published by Jossey-Bass Inc in association with The White Lion Press Limited. Softback, 169 pp. ISBN 978-0-7879-8314-7

If all that has ever been said and written about the art and science of fundraising could be distilled down to just what really matters there would be only a small number of true gems deserving of the description 'nuggets of information'.

Ken Burnett has identified and defined 89 such nuggets that he presents here as *The Zen of Fundraising* – a fun-to-read, one-of-a-kind look into what makes donors tick and, more importantly, what makes them give.

'Ken Burnett knows what donors want and how fundraisers can provide it. *The Zen of Fundraising* illustrates simple yet hard-earned lessons through which fundraisers can engage their donors as real partners, raising more money than ever. But to succeed, fundraisers need to aspire to greater levels of communication and donor engagement. This books shows us how.'
Chuck Longfield, founder and CEO, Target Software Inc, USA.

'The refreshingly brief principles provide inspiration and learning to anyone striving for exceptional fundraising practice.'
Nicci Dent, director of fundraising, Médecins sans Frontières, Australia.

'A gentle blend of humour, personal experiences and practical examples (but underpinned by pure steel), this book makes the most compelling case yet for thinking about donor relationships.'
Adrian Sargeant, adjunct professor of philanthropy, Indiana University Center on Philanthropy, USA.

Relationship Fundraising: A Donor-based Approach to the Business of Raising Money (second edition)

by Ken Burnett
Published by Jossey-Bass Inc in association with
The White Lion Press Limited. Hardback, 384 pp.
ISBN 0-7879-6089-6

Ken Burnett has completely revised and updated his classic book *Relationship Fundraising*. Filled with illustrative case examples, donor profiles, and more than 200 action points, this groundbreaking book shows fundraisers how to:

• Implement creative approaches to relationship-building fundraising.

• Avoid common fundraising errors and pitfalls.

• Apply the vital ingredients for fundraising success.

• Build good relationships with donors through marketing.

• Achieve a greater understanding of donors.

• Communicate effectively with donors – using direct mail, the press, television, the telephone, face-to-face contact, and more.

• Prepare for the challenges of twenty-first century fundraising.

'Not since Harold Seymour's classic, *Designs for Fund Raising*, has a book of this magnitude come along.

'Ken Burnett's updated and expanded work, *Relationship Fundraising*, just may be the book to which fundraising professionals turn for the next several decades.

'It is as brilliant as it is heartfelt, as simple as it is eloquent.'
Jerry Cianciolo, *The Compleat Professional's Library*, *Contributions Magazine*, USA.

'Ken Burnett's observations, insights and practical tips for building and sustaining relationships are superb. Highly readable, this book is a solid mix of sound theory and pragmatic application.'
Kay Sprinkel Grace, author, *Beyond Fund Raising*; co-author *High Impact Philanthropy*, USA.

'This is the book that sets the agenda for fundraising communications in the

twenty-first century. Engaging, inspiring, and thought-provoking, *Relationship Fundraising* is based on the unique 25-year experience of one of the world's most respected fundraisers.'
Bernard Ross, director, The Management Centre, UK; co-author, *Breakthrough Thinking for Nonprofit Organizations.*

Friends for Life: Relationship Fundraising in Practice

by Ken Burnett
Hardback, 599 pp. ISBN 0-9518971-2-8

Amid the widespread acclaim that greeted the 1992 publication of Ken Burnett's *Relationship Fundraising* was one persistent qualified comment. Essentially the question was 'relationship fundraising sounds very attractive, but will it help us raise more money?'

In this accessible and entertaining sequel, Ken Burnett describes how relationship fundraising is working in a wide variety of organisations in the USA, Canada and the United Kingdom. Their stories provide the answer: a loud and resounding 'yes!'

But the ideas and experiences described in this book will do much more than just help fundraisers raise more money. They will show them how to develop and maintain strong, healthy, mutually beneficial relationships with their donors; relationships that will enable them to make friends for life.

The sequel to *Relationship Fundraising* first appeared in 1996, to international acclaim.

'I'm an enthusiastic fan of Ken Burnett's approach to building friends for life. His new book builds on the practical, common-sense approach to donor development he is famous for advocating.

'Great examples, an easy read – I highly recommend *Friends for Life: Relationship Fundraising in Practice.*'
Dr Judith E Nichols, CFRE, author and consultant, USA.

'*Friends for Life* is a witty, readable tour of donor-think from both sides of the Atlantic and brings together a unique collection of experiences and anecdotes from many world-class fundraisers. *Relationship Fundraising* is already a classic throughout the world and this sequel is sure to have a similar impact.'
Jennie Thompson, consultant and co-founder of Craver, Mathews, Smith and Company, USA.

'The Botton Village case history is riveting. Its lessons have a relevance beyond fundraising. This is what direct marketing should always be, but so seldom is.'
Graeme McCorkell, author and consultant, UK.

Asking Properly: The Art of Creative Fundraising

by George Smith
Hardback, 220 pp.
ISBN 0-9518971-1-X

You will never read a book quite like this. George Smith tears open the conventional wisdom of fundraising creativity and so changes the rules for an entire trade. This book is irreverent, funny, savagely critical and genuinely inspiring, often on the same page.

Asking Properly is almost certainly the most authoritative book ever written about the creative aspects of fundraising. It is likely to remain a key text for years to come.

The author offers a profound analysis of donor motivation and is critical of the extent to which charities take their supporters for granted. But this book is no mere commentary on current practice – it offers a comprehensive checklist on how to optimise the creative presentation of the fundraising message. How to write, design, use direct mail, press advertising, broadcast media and the telephone, how to think in terms of fundraising products... the whole gallery of creativity and media is surveyed and assessed, with hundreds of examples of fundraising campaigns from around the world illustrating the need to 'ask properly'.

The book will prove invaluable to anyone involved in the

fundraising process. It is provocative, entertaining and, above all, highly instructive. Read it, apply its lessons and it must enable you to raise more money.

'This book will become a classic. It's not just inspirational and a great read, there's a practical benefit on every page. When you apply George Smith's secrets you can hardly fail to improve your fundraising.'
Harvey McKinnon, president, Harvey McKinnon Associates, Canada.

'It's typically George Smith: wise, uncompromising, devastatingly critical of poor fundraising, brilliantly illustrative of what is good, full of ideas, funny, marvellously written – and exceptionally good value. In short, *Asking Properly* is one of those very few books you will keep for life.'
Pierre-Bernard Le Bas, vice-present, fundraising and communication, Christian Blind Mission, France.